BIBLE HANDBOOK

A classic Bible-study guide

S. N. Haskell

Author of
*The Story of Daniel the Prophet, The Story of the
Seer of Patmos, The Cross and Its Shadow*

REVIEW AND HERALD® PUBLISHING ASSOCIATION
Since 1861 | www.reviewandherald.com

ISBN 978-0-8280-0556-2

9 780828 005562

Printed by Pacific Press® Publishing Association

Printed in U.S.A.
To order additional copies, call 1-800-765-6955

November 2017

... presented in this book, with other Bible studies not previously printed.

For lack of space we have given simply groups of texts on some subjects. In many of the Bible studies reference is given to the works of Mrs. E. G. White. These references give additional light upon the subjects under consideration.

The Bible Handbook contains over 220 Bible studies and groups of texts. We send it forth with the prayer that it may aid many in becoming better acquainted with the Book of all books,—the Bible, thus encouraging them to become soul-winners for their Lord and Master.

S. N. H.

Abbreviations for titles of books referred to in the Bible Handbook.

G. C. Great Controversy Between Christ and Satan

P. P. Patriarchs and Prophets

P. K. The Story of Prophets and Kings

D. A. The Desire of Ages

A. A. The Acts of the Apostles

M. H. Ministry of Healing

C. O. L. Christ's Object Lessons

C. T. Christian Temperance

E. W. Early Writings

G. W. Gospel Workers

L. S. Life Sketches

E. Education

T. Testimonies for the Church

v. Volume

by the Holy Ghost, having no control of the work themselves. They penned the literal truth, and stern, forbidding facts are revealed for reasons that our finite minds cannot fully comprehend." T., v. 4, p. 9.

Magnifying the Word of God

Phil. 2:9, 10. At the name of Jesus every knee in heaven and earth shall bow.

Ps. 138:2. The Lord magnifies His word above all His name.

Ps. 119:89. God's word is forever settled in heaven.

Ps. 12:6; Prov. 30:5. "The words of the Lord are pure words: as silver tried in a furnace of earth, purified seven times." E. 244.

Matt. 4:4, 7, 10. The Saviour was fortified against temptation by the written word. He used nothing except what we have within our reach. D. A. 123-126; T., v. 5, p. 434.

1 Peter 1:22-25. The new birth comes by the word of God. P. K. 626.

1 Peter 2:2, 3. As new-born babes we should desire the sincere milk of the word that we may grow thereby.

Ps. 119:9. The word will cleanse the life. C. O. L. 110, 111.

Ps. 119:133. Our steps should be ordered by the word. M. H. 458.

Matt. 4:4. It is as essential as our daily food. T., v. 4, p. 499.

2 Cor. 3:1-3. Unbelievers read the Bible in the lives of God's people.

1 Peter 3:1. They "may without the word" be converted by the godly lives of earnest Christians.

Power of the Word

Heb. 4:12. All the power of God is in His word. E. 254, 255.

Jer. 23:29. "Is not my word like as a fire? saith the Lord; and like a hammer that breaketh the rock in pieces?" T., v. 5, pp. 24, 25.

Ps. 33:6-9; Heb. 11:1-3. "By the word of the Lord were the heavens made; and all the host of them by the breath of His mouth." E. 125, 126.

Ps. 107:20. There is healing power in the word of God.

Matt. 8:8-13. One word from Christ brought health to the sick. D. A. 316, 317.

Ps. 103:3. God heals all diseases.

Prov. 4:20-22, margin. The words of God are medicine to those who receive them. M. H. 466.

John 1:1. The words that God speaks are synonymous with Himself. T., v. 4, p. 312.

Christi), and the Holy G

1 Tim. 3:16. This union is a mystery that human minds cannot comprehend.

Deut. 10:4, margin. Each one of the commandments is a word, or a complete thought.

Heb. 4:12. God's word is a discerner of the thoughts and intents of the heart.

Ps. 119:11. Hid in the heart, it will shield from sin.

Matt. 8:9, 10. Great faith is simply to believe, because God speaks. E. 257.

Deut. 8:3. When deprived of every earthly resource, we learn to live upon the word of God. P. K. 428.

1 John 5:4. Faith in the Word as the word of God, carries the transforming power of God to the soul. T., v. 4, pp. 545, 546.

How to Read and Study the Bible

Neh. 8:8. Whether reading alone or before others, pronounce every word distinctly, giving the sense. T., v. 6, pp. 380-383.

Luke 10:26. Jesus laid as much stress on the reading of the Scriptures as on what they contained. G. C. 598.

2 Tim. 2:7. "Consider *what I say*; and the Lord

give thee understanding in all things." E. 189.

Dan. 10:11. "Understand the *words* that I speak unto thee." G. C. 599, 600.

Matt. 28:20. The disciples' commission was to teach what *Christ had commanded*.

2 Tim. 4:2. Paul charged Timothy to preach the Word. A. A. 506.

Rev. 22:18; Prov. 30:5, 6. No one is to add to, or take from, the words of God. God has expressed the thoughts He intended to convey, and we are to study the words and get from them the thoughts He designed to convey when He gave the words. E. 227.

Jer. 23:28. Man's words are but chaff when compared with the words of God. A. A. 474, 475.

How to Teach the Word of God

1 Cor. 2:13. The Holy Ghost's method of teaching is by comparing spiritual things with spiritual.

John 5:39. Christ commands us to search the Scriptures. D. A. 390.

Luke 24:25-27, 44, 45. He appeals to the Scriptures to prove His resurrection.

John 10:34-36. Jesus teaches that the omission of one letter, making the word singular when the prophet had used the plural form, would break the Scriptures.

Gal. 3:16. The apostle Paul holds the same view of the Scriptures.

2 Sam. 23:2. David says that the Lord's "*word* was in my tongue."

the word of God, he lost his kingdom. 1. 1. 634-636.

1 Sam. 15:22, 23. It is as the sin of witchcraft to think that God's words can be changed. The entire fifteenth chapter of 1 Samuel should be studied carefully. P. P. 680-682.

DUTY

"Our duty will only be discerned and appreciated when viewed in the light which shines from the life of Christ." T., v. 3, p. 403.

Our Duty to God

Job 23:12. We should esteem God's word above food.

Deut. 6:5; Luke 10:27. Love God with all the heart, soul, mind, and strength. T., v. 8, p. 139.

1 Sam. 12:24; Rom. 12:11. Serve Him with the whole heart.

1 Cor. 6:19, 20. Glorify God in our bodies.

Matt. 6:24; Luke 14:33. Give Him unreserved service.

Mark 8:34. Deny self and take up our cross daily.

Matt. 19:21, 28, 29. Give all for Christ.

Rev. 3:16. Want of full consecration condemned.

Ex. 22:29; Prov. 3:9. Honor God with our substance. T., v. 4, pp. 76, 77.

1 Thess. 2:12. Walk worthy of God.

1 Cor. 10:31. Do all to God's glory.

Our Duty to the Nation

Rom. 13:1. God ordained the nations.

Matt. 22:19-21. Render the nation all the honor that belongs to it.

Rom. 13:1. Be subject to the nation. T., v. 1, pp. 361, 201, 202.

Rom. 13:1, 2. Disrespect for the just claims of the nation is showing disrespect to God.

Rom. 13:3, 4. Nations are ministers under God for good.

Dan. 4:13-18; 10:20; 11:1. Angels watch over the nations. T., v. 1, p. 203.

1 Tim. 2:1-3. Pray for the rulers of the nation.

Prov. 8:15, 16. God establishes national rulers.

Acts 5:29. When nations step over the boundary and enforce laws contrary to God's requirements, then the Christian should always obey God rather than men.

SECOND ADVENT OF CHRIST

"THE doctrine of the second advent is the very key-note of the Sacred Scriptures. From the day the first pair turned their sorrowing steps from Eden, the children of faith have waited the coming of the Promised One to break the destroyer's power and bring them again to the lost Paradise." G. C. 299.

...the angels. D. A. 759.

Matt. 17:2. Christ's glory,—face as the sun, raiment as light. A. A. 33.

Eze. 1:28. The Father's glory like the rainbow.

Ex. 24:16, 17. God's glory like devouring fire to the wicked.

Matt. 28:2, 3. The glory of one angel.

Matt. 28:4. The effect of that glory.

Matt. 25:31. All the angels come with Christ.

Rev. 5:11. Compare the effect of one with the whole company of angels.

Rev. 6:15-17. Wicked seek to hide.

2 Thess. 1:8, 9; 2:8. Effect upon the wicked.

Jer. 25:30-33. Wicked slain.

Luke 17:26-30. Compared with the time of Noah and Lot. P. P. 90-95, 156-161.

Matt. 28:5. No fear for those who seek Jesus. G. C. 641.

1 Thess. 4:16, 17. The righteous caught up.

1 Cor. 15:51-53. Made immortal. D. A. 320.

Phil. 3:20, 21. Bodies like Christ's.

Matt 17:2. Faces like the sun.

Matt. 13:43. Shine as the sun in the kingdom of their Father.

Luke 21:34-36. Preparation for His coming. T., v. 4, pp. 306, 307.

Effect of Christ's Coming on the Earth, or the Millennium

Isa. 2:17-21. Earth terribly shaken. E. W. 272.

Rev. 6:14-17. Every mountain and island moved. E. W. 285.

Rev. 16:17-21. Greatest earthquake that has ever been.

Isa. 24:1, 3-6. Earth utterly emptied. E. W. 289, 290.

1 Thess. 4:13-17. Righteous taken.

Jer. 25:33. Wicked slain.

Jer. 4:23-27; Zeph. 1:2, 3. Earth wholly desolate.

Rev. 20:1-3. Satan bound; no one to tempt. E. W. 290.

Rev. 20:4-6. Wicked live again after a thousand years.

Rev. 20:7, 8. Satan loosed.

Rev. 20:9, 10. Wicked gather about the city and are destroyed. C. O. L. 318, 319.

2 Peter 3:7-13. Same fire purifies the earth. E. W. 295.

Leave the reader with the thought of the new earth. Avoid controversy about the fate of the wicked.

New Earth

Ps. 115:16. Earth given to the children of men. P. P. 44-49.

Gen. 1:27, 28. Adam and Eve given dominion.

Gen. 3:1-6. Man fell.

Rom. 6:16. In yielding they lost the dominion. P. P. 55-61.

John 14:30. Satan prince of this world.

Gal. 3:29. Heirs to the earth.

2 Peter 3:7-13. Earth purified.

Isa. 65:17. New earth promised.

Rev. 21:1. A new earth.

Isa. 51:3. Made like Eden.

Isa. 35:1-10. Description of new earth. G. C. 674-676.

Isa. 65:21-25. Employment on the new earth. E. W. 18.

Isa. 33:24. Inhabitants never sick.

Rev. 21:4. No pain nor death. T., v. 9, p. 287.

Isa. 66:22, 23. Regular seasons of worship.

Matt. 5:5. Meek will inherit the earth.

Capital City of the New Earth

Rev. 21:1, 2. Holy city descends upon the earth. E. W. 18, 291.

Rev. 21:9-11. The city the bride.

Rev. 21:12, 13. Angel gate-keepers.

Rev. 21:21. Gates of pearl.

Rev. 21:18. Wall of jasper.

Rev. 21:18. City of pure gold.

Rev. 21:21. Streets of gold.

Rev. 21:16. Size of the city.

Rev. 21:19, 20. Twelve foundations garnished with all manner of stones.

Rev. 21:23. No need of sun in the city.

Isa. 24:23. Glory of Christ puts sun to shame. G. C. 676.

Isa. 30:26. Sun seven times brighter than now.

Rev. 21:24. Gather in the city from all over the world.

Rev. 22:1, 2. The tree of life with twelve manner of fruits. E. W. 289.

Isa. 66:22, 23. Gather monthly and partake of the fruit.

Rev. 21:8. Fearful and unbelieving never enter.

Rev. 22:14. Obedient enter the city.

New Earth as Taught in the Sanctuary Service No. 1

Gen. 3:17. The Lord said unto Adam: "Cursed is the ground for thy sake." Adam's sin affected the earth.

Isa. 24:5. "The earth also is defiled under the inhabitants thereof."

Gen. 4:9-11. There must be some remedy to meet the demand, and free the earth from the curse.

Num. 35:33. The only way the land can be freed from the curse is through the offering of the blood of the same race that brought the sin upon the earth. E. W. 126, 127.

Neh. 5:4, 5. Man is powerless to redeem the earth from the curse of sin.

Mark 3:26, 27. Satan is prince of this world. Some one stronger than Satan must arise to destroy him and remove the curse.

.... that
...... be sold. If one became
involved, the land passed into the hands of another, the one "near of kin" could redeem it.
P. P. 534.

Heb. 2:17. Christ partook of the nature of man, became our brother, one "near of kin," that He
might deliver us and pay the redemption price
for the earth. D. A. 327.

Eph. 1:13, 14. The future inheritance of the saints
is called "the *purchased* possession"; it has
been bought by the precious blood of Christ.

Lev. 4:7, 18, 25, 30. In every sin-offering, after
the atonement was made for the sinner, the
remainder of the blood was poured on the
ground at the bottom of the brazen altar, thus
signifying that the blood of Christ would
cleanse the *land* from the curse of sin.

Lev. 6:9-11. As the ashes accumulated on the altar,
they were carefully collected and carried forth
and put in a "clean place."

Ps. 37:20; 73:12-18. The burning of those offerings typified the destruction of all sin and sinners in the lake of fire.

Mal. 4:1-3. When the fire of the last days has de-

stroyed sin and sinners and purified the earth,
the saints will walk over the ashes of the
wicked on a "clean place,"—the earth made
new.

Lev. 6:10. In the type the priest changed his
garments before he carried the ashes to the
"clean place."

Rev. 19:11-16. Christ lays aside His priestly robes
and clothes Himself in kingly garments when
He comes to destroy the wicked.

New Earth as Taught in the Sanctuary Service No. 2

Jer. 9:21. The air is laden with death and disease.

Ex. 15:23. Water is contaminated by the curse of
sin.

Gen. 3:17. The land, air, and water all share in
the curse of sin.

Lev. 14:1-17. The offering for the cleansing of the
leper included the cleansing of the earth, air,
and sea, from the curse of sin.

Lev. 14:7. The blood of the sacrifice was sprinkled
upon the leper, thus typifying the blood of
Christ which cleanses man from sin.

Lev. 14:5, 6. Two birds were chosen; one was slain
over running *water*, and the blood was caught
in an *earthen* vessel; thus the blood came in
contact with water and earth, typifying the
blood of Christ which will purify the earth
and sea.

Lev. 14:6, 7. The living bird, after being dipped
in the blood, was let loose, bearing through the
air the blood of cleansing, thus typifying that
the blood of Christ will remove every taint of

... again clothe the earth in Edenic beauty.

Signs of Christ's Coming in the Heavens

Luke 21:25, 26. There shall be signs in the heavens and earth.

Joel 3:15. Sun, moon, and stars darkened. G. C. 306-308.

Rev. 6:12. Sun black as sackcloth.

Isa. 13:10. Sun darkened in its going forth,—morning.

Amos 8:9. Darkest at noon, in a clear sky.

Eze. 32:7. Sun covered with cloud.

Amos 5:8. Night also dark.

Rev. 6:12. Moon like blood.

Matt. 24:29. Immediately after the tribulation of the 1260 years.

Mark 13:24. Darkened *in the days,* but after the tribulation.

Matt. 24:22. Days were shortened.

Tribulation ceased about 1776. The 1260 years of Dan. 7:25 began 538 A. D. and ended 1798. The signs in the sun and moon were to be seen between the end of the tribulation and 1798 A. D. An account of the fulfillment is given in Webster's Dictionary, 1869 edition, as follows:—

"The Dark Day, May 19, 1780,—so called on account of the remarkable darkness on that day extending all over New England. In some places, persons could not see to read common print in the open air for several hours together. . . . The obscuration began at about ten o'clock in the morning, and continued till the middle of the next night, but with differences of degree and duration in different places. For several days previously the wind had been variable, but chiefly from the southwest and northeast. The true cause of this remarkable phenomenon is not known."

Herschel, the astronomer, says:—

"The Dark Day in North America was one of those wonderful phenomena of nature which will always be read of with interest, but which philosophy is at a loss to explain."

Rev. 6:13. Stars fell as green fruit. G. C. 333, 334.

An entire chapter in Deven's "Our First Century," pp. 329-336, is devoted to the description of the great shower of stars of Nov. 13, 1833, which fulfilled this prophecy in every respect.

Luke 21:28-31. The signs *began* to come to pass in 1780, and now they *have come to pass.*

Matt. 24:33, margin. Saviour at the door.

Luke 21:32; Matt. 24:34. This generation shall not pass till all these things are fulfilled. D. A. 632.

It must be either the generation addressed by the Saviour or the generation that saw the signs fulfilled.

Luke 11:29. The generation living in Christ's day had only *one* sign, and therefore could not

Matt. 24:7, 8. Earthquake and pestilence. T., v. 8, p. 252; v. 7, p. 11.

Luke 21:25. Distress of nations.

Matt. 24:7. Nation against nation. T., v. 9, pp. 14-28.

Mark 13:7, 8. Wars and rumors of wars. P. K. 278.

Joel 3:9, 10. Prepare war; beat plowshares into swords.

Joel 3:11, 12. Heathen nations awaken.

Jer. 25:26-28. All kingdoms of the world will be drawn into war.

Isa. 8:9, 10. Trusts and combines broken.

Isa. 8:12-14. Righteous principles will endure.

Important Signs of the Last Days

Dan. 12:4. Knowledge increased; much traveling.

Jas. 5:1-3. Riches heaped together. G. C. 654.

Ps. 49:11. Hope their houses will continue forever.

Jas. 5:4. Laboring man oppressed.

Nahum 2:3. "In the days of His preparation" the chariots have flaming torches,—great headlights.

Nahum 2:5. A description of the conductor of any rapid train of cars, as he recounts his passengers and collects fares.

Nahum 2:4. Automobiles running like lightning and raging in the streets.

Nahum 3:16, 17. One who has lived in the countries where locusts abound and has seen the sun darkened for hours by dense clouds of locusts flying so high they could scarcely be distinguished from the clouds, can readily think the prophet saw the "merchant," "crowned" ones and "captains" soaring in airplanes "as the locusts."

Isa. 8:19. Spiritualism will increase. E. W. 263.

Rev. 16:13-15. Strongly manifested in powers of earth.

Rev. 16:14. Devil power to work miracles. T., v. 9, p. 16.

2 Cor. 11:14, 15. Power to personate individuals. G. C. 552.

Isa. 8:20. Word of God the supreme test.

Last Day Signs in Spiritual World

Matt. 24:24. False prophets arise.

Luke 17:26-28. Feasting and revelry. T., v. 3, pp. 164, 165.

Isa 22:12-14. Flesh-eating and drunkenness. T., v. 9, pp. 153-157.

Isa. 66:15-17. Those who do not control their appetites destroyed. T., v. 9, pp. 159, 160.

1 Tim. 4:1. Some depart from the faith.

1 Tim. 4:3. These apostates strive to turn others from God's original diet. Gen. 1:29.

Matt. 24:48, 49. Evil servants say the Lord delays His coming.

2 Tim. 3:1. The last days perilous times. C. O. L. 228.

Joel 3:10. The Lord, ...
that day.

Three Comings of Christ and the Marriage
of the Lamb

THERE are three separate positions taken in regard to the advent of Christ; 1st, He comes to judge the world; 2nd, He comes as a thief; 3rd, He comes to take His people to heaven. There is truth in each position, for they do not relate to the same event but to three separate events which take place in their order.

Coming of Judgment, or Going to the
Marriage

Mal. 3:1-5. Christ will suddenly come to judgment.

Dan. 7:9, 10, 13, 14; Matt. 25:10. Christ went to the marriage when He went to the judgment. G. C. 427.

Rev. 21:9, 10. The New Jerusalem, the bride.

Isa. 62:4. The land is married, becomes the bride.

2 Cor. 11:2; Isa. 54:5; Eph. 5:23. The church is the bride. Christ is married to the *city*, the *land*, and the *church*.

Dan. 7:13, 14. Christ brought before the Father to

receive His kingdom. It takes four things to
make a kingdom: viz., territory, people, capital,
or seat of government, and a king. The giving
of the *city, people* and *land* to Christ, the *King,*
constitutes the marriage.

Luke 19:12. Christ has gone into a far country to
receive a kingdom. T., v. 8, p. 37.

Dan. 7:9, 10. Judgment precedes the marriage, as
it must be determined who are the subjects of
the kingdom before they are given to Christ.
G. C. 428.

Matt. 22:2, 8-14. The judgment is compared to the
examination of wedding garments. G. C. 427.

Matt. 25:1-10. All that are ready will have on the
wedding garment. C. O. L. 406, 407.

Rev. 19:7, 8. The necessary garment is the white
robe of righteousness.

Isa. 61:10. The garments are provided; guests have
only to accept them.

Rev. 3:5. They are given to the overcomers.

Coming as a Thief, or the Marriage

Matt. 24:42-44. One coming of the Lord is compared
to a thief; no one knows when a thief comes
until after he has done his work and gone. T.,
v. 6, p. 129; v. 9, p. 135.

Dan. 7:13, 14; Rev. 22:11, 12. When the judgment
closes and Christ receives the kingdom, the decree is given which forever determines the destiny of every soul on earth. But He comes as
a thief; none know when they pass the line
which forever closes probation. G. C. 491; T.,
v. 2, pp. 190-193.

... wrath of ... poured out.

Hab. 3:2. Previous to this time mercy is mingled with all the judgments of God. E. W. 281.

Ps. 75:7, 8. The wicked drink the dregs.

Heb. 11:16. Christ has prepared the city.

Dan. 7:13, 14. The city and subjects are all ready when the kingdom is given to Christ, but the land is still occupied by the enemy.

Christ Coming for His People, or Coming from the Wedding

Luke 19:15. After having received the kingdom Christ returns to the earth. E. W. 251, 280.

Luke 12:35-37. This is also called returning from the wedding.

Matt. 13:38-41. Having received the kingdom, He comes to set it in order, and remove all trace of sin. E. W. 55.

Rev. 19:16. Christ comes in kingly robes.

Rev. 20:1-9. It takes over 1000 years to destroy the last trace of sin from the earth.

Rev. 20:4. During this time the saints are with Christ.

1 Thess. 4:16. When Christ comes for His people, He remains in the clouds. E. W. 286, 287.

Zech. 14:4. At the end of 1000 years His feet will touch on the Mount of Olives, and the work of purifying the earth begins. E. W. 291.

Rev. 21:9, 10. The city descends.

Rev. 20:9. Fire from God devours the wicked. E. W. 294.

2 Peter 3:7-13. The same fire purifies the earth.

2 Peter 3:5-7. As the earth was once cleansed from sin by water, so it will again be cleansed by fire.

Nahum 1:9. Sin arose again after the flood; but after the fires have done their work, it will never rise up again a second time.

Isa. 33:14, 15; Gen. 8:1. As Noah rode in safety on the waters of the flood, so the righteous in the city of God will dwell safely in the midst of the fire. G. C. 673.

Isa. 35:1-10. Earth purified,—clad in wedding garments.

Rev. 19:9. Then will come the marriage supper. E. W. 19.

Luke 12:37. Christ Himself will serve.

Close of Probation

Eze. 9:3, 4. The work of placing the mark, or seal, upon God's children entrusted to one angel.

Rev. 7:1-3. The sealing message is the most important work on earth, and nothing is to retard it.

Eze. 9:11, margin. When the work is completed, the angel returns to God with the words, "I have done as thou hast commanded me." G. C. 613.

of life.

Dan. 12:1; 11:20, 21. The term "stand up," indicates that Michael (Christ) at this time ceases to be high priest, and takes His kingdom and is called "King of kings" from that time forward.

1 Tim. 2:5. Christ is the only mediator between God and man; and when He ceases to be priest there is no one to plead for guilty man. E. W. 280.

Rev. 14:8-10. When there is no mediator in the heavens, there is nothing to prevent the wrath of God from being poured out upon the wicked.

Isa. 59:16-18; Lev. 16:23. Christ puts on the garments of vengeance.

Rev. 15:1. The work of pouring out the unmixed wrath of God upon the earth is assigned to seven angels, and is called the seven last plagues.

Rev. 15:8; 1 Tim. 2:5. "The *man* Christ Jesus" can not enter the temple while the seven last plagues are being poured out upon the earth.

Ex. 8:20-23, margin. The Lord sent ten plagues upon Egypt; the first three plagues fell upon the Israelites as well as upon the Egyptians, but none of the seven last plagues of Egypt fell upon the

children of Israel. Ex. 8:22; 9:4-7, 26; 10:23;
G. C. 627, 628.

Ps. 91:1-10. Likewise, when the psalmist foretold the
effect of the seven last plagues, he said no
plague would come nigh the dwelling of the
righteous. G. C. 630.

Seven Last Plagues

Rev. 16:1. The seven angels pour out the vials of
God's wrath upon the earth. G. C. 628, 629.

Rev. 16:2. The first plague is a "noisome and
grievous sore."

Rev. 16:3. The second plague causes the sea to become "as the blood of a dead man."

Rev. 16:4. The third plague causes the rivers and
fountains of water to become blood.

Rev. 16:5, 6. After the plagues have affected all the
water upon the earth, the angel of the waters
declares it to be a righteous judgment.

Rev. 16:7. An angel from heaven responds.

Rev. 16:8. The fourth plague will cause the sun
to "scorch men with fire."

Rev. 16:9. These plagues will cause men to blaspheme God; naturally they accuse God's people, who are sheltered from the plagues, as being responsible for the plagues.

Rev. 16:10. The fifth plague is darkness that fills
all the kingdom of the beast. C. O. L. 420.

Rev. 16:11. The wicked are still suffering because
of the sores that come under the first plague,
and they blaspheme God and continue to
blame God's people for all the plagues that
have fallen upon them. If they blaspheme God,
naturally they will hate His representatives.

Rev. 16:13. Aside from the people of God, there remain three classes; "the dragon," the power which sought to destroy the child Jesus, or paganism (Rev. 12:1-5); "the beast," which persecuted the church during the 1260 years (the period known in history as the Dark Ages); and "the false prophet," or apostate Protestantism.

Rev. 16:13, 14. Spiritualism takes control of all three of these classes and unites them in a war against God and His people. T., v. 5, p. 451.

Rev. 16:15; Isa. 33:14. Those who are holy and righteous are protected and blessed; while those who are classed with the people of God, but are not really of them at this time, are fully revealed.

Rev. 13:15. The decree goes forth that all who do not worship the beast will be slain. Esther 3: 13-15; G. C. 635; E. W. 282.

Seventh Plague

Rev. 16:16, 17. When all plans are laid to destroy the people of God from the earth, the seventh angel pours out his vial into the air; and God the Father from His throne in the temple says, "It is done." No longer will the powers of the earth be allowed to afflict the people of God. G. C. 636.

Rev. 16:18-20. The voice of God causes a great earthquake. The whole earth heaves and swells like the waves of the sea. E. W. 285.

Dan. 12:2. A partial resurrection takes place at this time. G. C. 637.

Isa. 30:27, 28. God puts "a bridle in the jaws of the people." They are powerless to carry out their murderous schemes, and are afraid of the righteous.

Ex. 11:4-8. It was about midnight that the last plague of Egypt was poured out upon the Egyptians. Before the angel passed through Egypt at midnight, the Israelites were slaves; after midnight the Egyptians bowed down to the Israelites and Israel was free. G. C. 636.

Job 34:20. At midnight "the mighty shall be taken away without hands."

Rev. 16:21; Job 38:22, 23. The great hailstones of the seventh plague fall on every side and destroy the cities of the earth.

Isa. 30:29. While the earth is heaving under the feet of the righteous, their voices ascend to heaven in song.

Psalm 46. This Psalm seems to have been written for this special occasion when mountain chains are sinking and inhabited islands disappearing. It is the song the righteous will sing. G. C. 639.

Job 22:30. Islands inhabited by the righteous will

eration which saw the signs would not pass
away before His coming, He said that none
but the Father knew the day and hour of
Jesus' coming; then He said, "But as the days
of Noah were, *so shall* also the coming of the
Son of man be."

Gen. 6:3-7; 7:1-7. Noah was given a period of 120
years to prepare the ark; but the *day* when the
flood would come was not revealed to him until
God called him into the ark and an eternal line
of demarkation was placed between Noah and
his family and the wicked. Then the Lord said
that in seven days the flood would come; even
so, after God from heaven says, "It is done,"
and His people are forever free from the power
of the wicked, then He announces the day and
hour of Christ's coming. G. C. 640.

Matt. 24:30. The saints will know the day and hour
when the small cloud, the immediate sign of
Christ's coming, will appear. G. C. 640, 641.

Hab. 3:3, 4. Christ rides forth a mighty conqueror.
"His glory covers the heavens, and the earth
was full of His praise."

Rev. 19:11-14. He is escorted by all the hosts of
heaven. Matt. 25:31.

Rev. 19:16. "He hath on His vesture and on His thigh a name written, King of kings, and Lord of lords."

Rev. 6:14-16; Isa. 2:17-21. The wicked seek to hide from His presence. C. O. L. 421.

Isa. 25:9. The righteous rejoice at His coming.

Isa. 26:19. Christ looks upon the graves of the sleeping saints and cries, "Awake and sing, ye that dwell in the dust."

1 Cor. 15:51-55. The righteous dead come forth with the song, "O death, where is thy sting? O grave, where is thy victory?" The whole earth resounds with the tread of the innumerable multitude of the redeemed. The living righteous are changed in a moment from mortal to immortal.

Matt. 24:31; Ps. 50:5. The command is given to the angels, "Gather my saints together unto me."

2 Thess. 2:8; Jer. 25:30-33. The wicked are left dead upon the earth, and remain dead until the resurrection of damnation at the end of 1000 years. John 5:28, 29; Rev. 20:4, 5.

1 Thess. 4:16-18. The living righteous are caught up to meet the Lord in the air and will remain forever with Him.

MINISTRY OF ANGELS

"Every redeemed one will understand the ministry of angels in his own life. The angel who was his guardian from his earliest moment; the angel who watched his steps, and covered his head in the day of peril; the angel who was with him in the valley of the shadow of death, who marked his resting-place, who was the first to greet him in the

Ps. 8:4, 5; Heb. 2:2, 7. Man was made lower than the angels; therefore, angels are not men.

Heb. 1:7. Angels were made spirits.

1 Cor. 15:44-46. Because they are made spirits, it does not mean that they do not have bodies.

Eze. 10:12, margin. Angels have flesh, backs, and hands. They are real, tangible bodies.

Gen. 19:1-3. They ate and drank with Lot in Sodom.

Gen. 3:22-24. They were sent to guard the way of the tree of life before the first man died; therefore, they are an entirely different order of beings from man.

Num. 22:22-27. While they are invisible to the naked eye, yet God has opened the eyes of even animals to see them.

Num. 22:31-35. When God opens the eyes of men they can see the angels.

Rev. 1:1. Angels are sent to communicate God's messages to prophets.

Rev. 19:10. Could men see and sense the sacredness of these messengers of God, they would worship them.

The Work of Good and Evil Angels

John 8:44. Satan once abode in the truth, but he lost his first estate.

Jude 6. Other angels fell.

2 Peter 2:4. They sinned.

1 John 3:4. Disobeyed the law of God.

Rev. 12:7-9. Satan and evil angels cast from heaven.

Rev. 13:14; 16:14. Evil angels work miracles.

Job 1:6-19. Have power over the elements. T., v. 9, p. 93.

Ps. 103:20. Good angels excel in strength.

2 Chron. 32:21; 2 Kings 19:35. One loyal angel slew 185,000 men in one night.

Acts 12:23. Herod smitten by an angel.

Ps. 34:7. Good angels protect God's people. D. A. 142, 143.

Acts 5:19. Open prison doors.

Dan. 6:22. Animals subject to them.

Rev. 14:18. Have power over fire.

Rev. 21:12. Gate keepers. E. W. 39, 37.

Acts 8:26. They direct God's people.

Heb. 1:13, 14. All minister to humanity. T., v. 3, pp. 381, 516.

Matt. 18:10. Each child of God has a guardian angel. T., v. 3, p. 364.

Isa. 37:14-36; Dan. 9:20-23. Answer prayer. D. A. 112.

Dan. 4:13-17; 11:1; 10:20. Control the affairs of nations. E. 305.

Ex. 23:20-22. Went before Israel in the wilderness.

Acts 1:9-11. Escorted Jesus into heaven. T., v. 6, p. 309.

.... we pray and whether we give
alms or not. T., v. 3, pp. 363, 364.
Acts 10:5. Both our given and surname.
Acts 10:6. Where we lodge and our occupation.
Judges 13:3-14. How to instruct parents in training
their children. D. A. 517.
1 Kings 19:5-8. How to prepare food.
2 Kings 1:2, 3. Whether we inquire of spiritualist
mediums or not. D. A. 259.
2 Chron. 32:21. The rank or office men fill.
Gen. 16:7, 8. Names of servants and mistresses.
Eccl. 5:6. Take notice of words spoken. T., v. 3, p.
312; v. 5, p. 59.

Different Orders of Angels

Luke 1:19 Angels stand in the presence of God.
Matt. 18:10. Behold God's face.
Eze. 1:14. Move swiftly like lightning.
Rev. 5:11. More than 100,000,000.
Ps. 68:17. God's chariots composed of angels.
Isa. 6:2, 6. Seraphim have their work.
Ex. 25:16-18. The cherubim were at either end of
the mercy-seat.
Ps. 80:1. God dwells between the cherubim.
Eze. 28:14. Before his fall Satan was a covering
cherub.

Dan. 10:21. Gabriel is the angel of prophecy.

Rev. 14:18. One angel has power over fire.

Rev. 16:5. There is an angel of the waters.

Rev. 2:1, 8, 12, 18; 3:1, 7, 14. Seven angels have charge of the messages to the seven churches.

Rev. 7:1. Four angels control war.

Rev. 7:2; Eze. 9:2-4. Angel in charge of the sealing work.

Rev. 8:2. Seven angels in charge of the sounding of the seven trumpets.

Rev. 10:1-10. A mighty angel opened the little prophetic book.

Rev. 14:6-12. The last warning messages are in charge of three angels.

Rev. 15:1. Seven angels pour out the last plagues.

Rev. 18:1-3. The angel of the loud cry.

Matt. 25:31; Rev. 19:14. The angels are perfectly organized, appear like armies as they come with Christ.

Rev. 19:17. One angel calls the fowls to the great supper.

Rev. 20:1. To another is given the work of binding Satan.

Gabriel, the Angel of Prophecy

Luke 1:19. Stands in presence of God. D. A. 98, 99.

Dan. 9:21. Appeared in vision to Daniel.

Dan. 10:21. There is none but Michael, or Christ, that unite with Gabriel in revealing prophecy.

Rev. 1:1-3. Four steps in giving prophecy: 1st, God; 2nd, Christ; 3rd, angel; 4th, the prophet. D. A. 234.

Rev. 22:16, 6. Christ's own angel.

Luke 22:43; Matt. 28:2. Strengthened Him in the

Isa. 7:14; Luke 1:26-38. When the time came for the fulfillment of the prophecy, Gabriel announced the fact to one who should fulfill it.

Luke 1:5-20. Comes from the presence of God to the one interested in the fulfillment of prophecy.

Gen. 24:1-48. "His angel" goes before the one interested in carrying out the plan of God.

Rev. 22:9. The fellowservant of John, the prophets, and those who keep the sayings of Revelation. Gabriel is the servant and will go before the individual who will give his life to assist in fulfilling the prophecies of Revelation.

THE SANCTUARY

"Such subjects as the sanctuary, in connection with the 2300 days, the commandments of God and the faith of Jesus, are perfectly calculated to explain the past Advent movement and show what our present position is, establish the faith of the doubting, and give certainty to the glorious future. These, I have frequently seen, were the principal subjects on which the messengers should dwell." E. W. 63.

Type and Antitype

Heb. 9:1. Earthly sanctuary. P. P. 343.

Ex. 25:9, 40, margin; 1 Chron. 28:19. Made after divine models. P. P. 313, 343, 349.

Heb. 8:1-5. Earthly shadow of heavenly. P. P. 343.

Heb. 9:1-3. Two apartments in earthly. P. P. 348.

Heb 9:24. Two apartments in heavenly. E. W. 32, 251, 252; G. C. 414, 415.

Heb. 9:2; Ex. 25:37. Seven lamps in earthly. G. C. 412.

Rev. 4:5. Seven lamps of fire in heavenly. E. W. 251.

Ex. 30:1-6. Golden altar in earthly sanctuary. P. P. 348.

Rev. 8:1-4. Golden altar in heavenly. T., v. 8, p. 177.

Ex. 30:7, 8. Incense burned on earthly altar. G. C. 412.

Rev. 8:3, 4. Incense offered on heavenly. P. P. 353, 367; T., v. 8, p. 178.

Lev. 16:12, 13. Incense burned in censer in earthly.

Rev. 8:5. Incense burned in heavenly censer. E. W. 32, 256; T., v. 8, p. 178.

Ex. 40:22, 23. Table of showbread. P. P. 354; E. W. 251.

Heb. 9:3-5; Ex. 25:10-22. Ark in second apartment of earthly. P. P. 348, 349.

Rev. 11:19. Ark in heavenly sanctuary. E. W. 32; G. C. 415.

Deut. 10:1-5; Ex. 25:16. The ark in earthly sanctuary contained the law of God. E. W. 32, 33.

Heb. 5:4. Priests and ... ..

Heb. 5:5, 6. Christ appointed by the Father. D. A. 757.

Heb. 5:1. Priests offered gifts and sacrifices for sin.

Heb. 9:26-28. Christ put away sin by offering Himself. D. A. 25.

Service in the First Apartment of the Sanctuary

Rev. 11:19; Ps. 102:19. Heavenly temple. G. C. 489.

Heb. 6:20; 8:1, 2. Jesus priest in heavenly temple. E. W. 48.

Heb. 4:14, 15. We are the congregation. T., v. 6, p. 366; E. W. 55.

Heb 8:1-5. Service in earthly a shadow of heavenly. G. C. 420.

Heb. 9:26; Lev. 4:27-31; 16:30. Object of service was to put away sin. P. K. 684, 685.

Heb. 9:22. Without shedding of blood there is no remission of sin. E. W. 149.

Matt. 26:28. Christ's blood shed for the remission of sins. A. A. 552, 553.

Lev. 4:27, 28. Sinner brought a lamb.

Lev. 4:29; Num. 5:6, 7. Sin confessed over the lamb.

Lev. 4:5, 6. Blood presented before the Lord.

Lev. 10:16-18; 6:30. Flesh eaten by priest before the Lord when the blood was not taken into the sanctuary. Either blood or flesh of every sin-offering was taken into the sanctuary. This was a type of the real work. G. C. 418.

John 1:29. Christ is the real Lamb of God. A. A. 33.

1 Peter 2:24. Christ bore our sins in *His own body*, or flesh. D. A. 751.

Heb. 9:12. Christ entered the heavenly temple with His own blood. E. W. 38, 253; G. C. 430.

Heb. 9:6. This service continued throughout the year. G. C. 421, 430.

All of this service was an object-lesson to lift up the great Sin-bearer before the people.

Service in the Second Apartment of the Sanctuary

Heb. 9:7. Service in second apartment only one day in the year. P. P. 352, 355.

Lev. 16:2, 29, 30. Atonement made on the tenth day of the seventh month. All sin put away on that day.

Lev. 16:2-4, 11-14. Preparation of the priest for service.

Lev. 16:7, 8. Lots cast upon the two goats. G. C. 419.

Lev. 16:9, 15-19. The Lord's goat offered as a sin-offering. P. P. 355, 356.

Num. 29:7-11. Sin-offering offered on the day of atonement besides the sin-offering of atonement.

Lev. 16:18, 19. The last work performed by the

Lev. 16:10, 21. The sins are placed on the
scapegoat. G. C. 485.

Ps. 7:16. David understood that the sins would
come down upon the head of the evil one.

Lev. 16:22. The goat was led into the wilderness.
P. P. 355.

Rev. 22:11, 12. When our High Priest leaves the
sanctuary to come into the earthly court, every
case will have been decided for eternity. E. W.
36, 279, 280.

Rev. 20:1-3. Satan, the antitypical scapegoat, receives the sins of the righteous, and is left
upon the desolate earth. G. C. 658; E. W. 178,
280, 281.

The Lamb of God that taketh away the sins of
the world should be made the central thought of
every text.

Judgment

Lev. 16:29, 30. The sanctuary cleansed from the
confessed sins of the people on the day of
atonement. G. C. 480.

Heb. 9:23. The heavenly sanctuary will be cleansed.
G. C. 352.

Jer. 2:22. Every sin is written in heaven. G. C.
482.

Acts 3:19-21. The sins of the righteous will all

be blotted out. Every case will be decided before the sins are blotted out; this will be the cleansing of the heavenly sanctuary. G. C. 352, 611, 612.

1 Thess. 4:16, 17. Before Christ comes, a line is drawn between the righteous and the wicked. T., v. 2, p. 355.

Dan. 7:9-11. Daniel was shown earthly powers carrying forward their work while the judgment was in session in heaven.

Rev. 11:18, 19. John saw the nations angry during the judgment. L. S. 413, 421.

Acts 24:25. The judgment was still in the future in Paul's day; therefore, it must take place between Paul's day and the second coming of Christ.

Acts 17:31. Judgment appointed. Christ's resurrection a pledge of the judgment.

Rev. 14:6, 7. An angel announces the opening of the judgment.

Rev. 14:8-14. There were only two other messages to be given to the world. The work of cleansing the earthly sanctuary was not seen by the people; they accepted it by faith. The *real* work of judgment is in heaven. We follow our Priest by faith. P. P. 353; D. A. 166.

Rom. 2:12, 13; Eccl. 12:13, 14; Jas. 2:12; Ps. 96:13. The law of God is the standard in the judgment. G. C. 482.

Dan. 7:10. The judgment is an examination of books. G. C. 480.

Rev. 20:12. The people are judged by what is written in the books. G. C. 487.

1 Cor. 4:5. Counsels and thoughts of the heart.
E. W. 58.

1 Sam. 2:3. Every action weighed. P. K. 639.

Matt. 12:36. All idle words. D. A. 323.

Rev 20:13. Judged according to works. T., v. 6,
pp. 310, 311.

Jer. 2:22. Every sin written. G. C. 482.

Dan. 7:9, 10; Rev. 20:12. Judged out of the things
written in the books. C. O. L. 310.

1 Peter 4:17. Judgment begins with the righteous.
G. C. 480.

Luke 20:35; 1 Thess. 4:16, 17. Those "accounted
worthy" come up in the first resurrection.
G. C. 482.

Luke 21:34-36. The living righteous will also be
accounted worthy. G. C. 483; T., v. 6, p. 130.

Eccl. 7:27. To "account" is to consider one by one.
G. C. 490.

1 Cor. 4:3-5. We are not to judge one another, but
keep in mind the judgment of God. T., v. 8,
p. 85; v. 9, pp. 185, 186.

1 Kings 8:39. God only knows the heart. D. A.
58.

1 Cor. 11:31. If we "judge ourselves, we should not
be judged." D. A. 314.

1 Cor. 11:32. Chastening is to prepare us for the judgment. E. W. 67.

Rev. 3:5. Names of the righteous retained in the book of life. G. C. 490.

Books of Judgment

Dan. 7:10; Rev. 20:12. "The books were opened," showing there were more than one. E. W. 52.

Mal. 3:16-18. The book of remembrance records thoughts and victories gained. D. A. 637; G. C. 481.

Ps. 56:8. Our wanderings and tears of repentance are recorded in God's book. G. C. 481.

Ps. 87:4-6. Place of birth and influences that go to make up our characters.

Ps. 139:15, 16. The members of our body are written in the Lord's book.

Rom. 2:1-5. A man's life is written so accurately that if he professes one thing and lives another, he treasures up wrath against the day of wrath. G. C. 487.

Luke 10:19, 20. To be enrolled in the book of life is the highest honor given mortals. C. O. L. 299.

Phil. 4:3. Names of faithful workers recorded. D. A. 313, 638.

Ex. 32:33. Names of those who cling to sin will be removed. G. C. 483, 486.

Rev. 3:5. Names of the faithful retained. G. C. 484.

Rev. 13:8; 17:8. Wicked are not recorded. G. C. 483.

Rev. 20:15. None will be saved whose names are

666.

Judgment of the Wicked

Ps. 1:5. Wicked will not stand in the judgment.

1 John 3:4. The law detects the sinner. G. C. 639.

1 Tim. 5:24, 25. Unconfessed sins follow after and condemn the individual. C. O. L. 294.

Jude 6, 7. Past punishments illustrate the future. G. C. 22.

Matt. 11:20-24. Wicked cities will answer in the judgment.

2 Peter 2:4. Fallen angels reserved for judgment. E. W. 291.

2 Peter 2:9. Unjust reserved for judgment.

1 Cor. 6:2, 3. Saints assist in judging the wicked. G. C. 661; E. W. 54, 291.

Rev. 20:1-4. This judgment is during the 1000 years. E. W. 53.

Rev. 20:5-7. At end of thousand years wicked are raised. G. C. 661.

Ps. 2:7-9. They refused a mediator, now they meet a judge. D. A. 210; E. W. 292.

Ps. 149:5-9. The saints take part in the execution of the judgment. E. W. 52.

Mal. 4:1-3. Wicked are destroyed by fire. G. C. 672, 673.

Rev. 20:13. All judged by their works.

Rev. 20:12. All judged by the record in the books.

Luke 12:47, 48. There will be degrees of punishment. G. C. 673; E. W. 294, 295.

Eze. 28:17-19. Satan himself reduced to ashes. G. C. 673.

Rev. 21:1-5. A new earth after sin is destroyed. G. C. 675, 676.

The time of the opening of the judgment is given in the Bible study on the 2300 days, page 45.

The Eighth Chapter of Daniel

Dan. 8:1. The third year of Belshazzar, the last year of Babylon.

Dan. 8:2. Daniel in Elam when given the vision.

Dan. 8:3-14. Symbols given,—a ram, a rough goat, a little horn, and the 2300 days.

Dan. 8:15. Daniel sought for the meaning. P. K. 553.

Dan. 8:16. Gabriel commissioned to make him understand.

Dan. 8:20. Ram represented Medo-Persia.

Dan. 8:21. Goat a symbol of Greece.

Dan. 8:6, 7. Overthrow of Grecia by Medo-Persia.

Dan. 8:8, 22; 11:4. Grecia divided into four divisions.

Dan. 8:24, 25. The power following Grecia, which will be understood at the time of the end. Verse 17.

Dan. 8:26, 27. Gabriel began to explain the time

ened captivity.

The 2300 Days of Dan. 8:14

Dan 9:20, 21. Gabriel appeared while Daniel was praying. P. K. 556.

Dan. 9:22, 23. Came to give understanding. Daniel told to consider the vision.

Dan. 9:24. Gabriel begins where he left off in Dan. 8:26, and explains the 2300 days. P. K. 556.

Dan. 9:25. The period begins with the command to restore and build Jerusalem.

Ezra 6:14. It took three kings to complete the decree. G. C. 326, 327.

Ezra 1:1-4. The first part given by Cyrus 536 B. C. P. K. 558-578.

Ezra 6:1-12. The second part given by Darius, the Persian. P. K. 578-609.

Ezra 7:11-27. Artaxerxes completed the decree in 457 B. C. It required 79 years to complete the decree. P. K. 610-617.

Ezra 7:9. Nearly half of the year passed before the decree reached Jerusalem. It was 456 1-2 before the decree went into effect. G. C. 327, 398, 399.

Dan. 9:25. The 2300 days began when the decree

went into effect 456 1-2 b. c.; 70 weeks, or 490 years, were determined, or cut off for the Jews. The six definite things mentioned were all fulfilled by Christ within the 70 weeks. His death sealed the vision. He was anointed at His baptism, the heavenly sanctuary was anointed before Christ entered it with His blood to fulfill the type. Ex. 40:9-11.

Dan. 9:25. The 70 weeks were divided into seven, sixty-two, and one week. P. K. 698-700.

Num. 14:34; Eze. 4:6, margin. A day of prophetic time equals a year.

Gen. 29:27. Seven years equal a week of symbolic time.

Dan. 9:25. Seven weeks and 62 weeks, or 483 years, reached to Messiah. Subtracting 456 1-2 years from 483, leaves 26 1-2 a. d., or 27 a. d., the date for the Messiah. G. C. 327, 328.

John 1:41, margin. The Hebrew word Messiah in English is anointed; the 483 years reached to the Anointed One.

Acts 10:38. Jesus was anointed with the Holy Ghost.

Luke 3:21, 22, margin. This anointing took place at the baptism of Christ, a. d. 27. D. A. 111, 112.

Mark 1:9-15. Jesus, as He entered upon His ministry, announced that "the time *was* fulfilled." G. C. 327.

Dan. 9:26, 27. In the midst of the 70th week, Messiah "was to be cut off," and "cause the sacrifice to cease."

Dan. 9:27. He was to confirm the covenant for

the stoning of Stephen, and everywhere preaching the word. This was A. D. 34, the end of the 70 weeks. The gospel was no longer confined to the Jews. Seventy weeks, or 490 years, taken from the 2300 days, leaves 1810 years. The 70 weeks ended A. D. 34; 1810 added to A. D. 34 brings us to the autumn of 1844.

Dan. 8:14. In the autumn of 1844, at the end of the 2300 days, the cleansing of the heavenly sanctuary, or the investigative judgment, began in the heavenly sanctuary. G. C. 486.

The Position and Work of Our Heavenly High Priest

Heb. 8:1. Christ, our High Priest, at the right hand of the throne of God. M. H. 71.

Heb. 8:2. He ministers in the heavenly sanctuary. A. A. 552, 553.

Ex. 25:40, margin. Earthly sanctuary pattern of the heavenly.

Heb. 8:1-5. The service of earthly priests an example or shadow of Christ's work in heaven. By studying of earthly priests, we learn of Christ's work. L. S. 278.

Heb. 9:6. There was a *continual* service in the

first apartment of the earthly sanctuary. G. C. 418.

1 Chron. 6:49. The high priest officiated at the brazen altar in the court at the golden altar in first apartment, and did all the work of the place, most holy, or second apartment.

Ex. 30:7, 8. Aaron, the high priest, officiated twice *every day*, morning and evening, in the first apartment.

Ex. 30:8. It was a *perpetual* incense; hence, was replenished on the day of atonement the same as other days. P. P. 348.

Ex. 29:42, 43. God's visible presence was seen sometimes at the door of the first apartment, or tabernacle of the congregation.

Ex. 30:36; Num. 17:4; Ex. 40:34, 36. He also met with them in the second apartment.

Rev. 1:11-13. John saw Christ officiating in the first apartment of the heavenly sanctuary. A. A. 585, 586.

Rev. 8:3, 4. He also saw the prayers and incense being offered on the golden altar in the first apartment of the heavenly sanctuary. P. P. 356.

Rev. 4:2-5. John was shown the throne of God in heaven with the seven lamps of fire before it, and the seats of the twenty-four elders round about it. This was the first apartment.

1 Chron. 24:1-31. The common priests of the earthly priesthood were divided into twenty-four courses. This custom was followed to the time of Christ. Luke 1:8. There were twenty-four chief men sometimes called governors of the sanctuary. 1 Chron. 24:4. The twenty-

the first apartment.

Heb. 9:7. The high priest went alone into the second apartment.

Lev. 16:17. There was no man in the tabernacle of the congregation, or first apartment, when the high priest went in to officiate on the day of atonement.

Lev. 16:29, 30. The sanctuary was cleansed on the tenth day of the seventh month from all the sins that were "before the Lord," all that had been confessed.

During the year, the service had been confined to the first apartment: it was now carried into the second apartment. The high priest alone officiated in *both* apartments that day. The incense on the altar had to be kept burning, and, if necessary, sin-offerings were offered. Num. 29:7-11.

Lev. 16:2. God promised to meet with Aaron, the high priest, in the second apartment.

Dan. 7:9, 10. Daniel saw the thrones placed, or change positions, and the Father take His seat upon His throne for judgment. His attention was attracted to the "wheels of burning fire" as the throne was moved from the 1st to the 2nd apartment of the heavenly sanctuary. E. W. 54, 55.

Eze. 1:1-27; 10:1-20. God's throne is a movable
throne.

Dan. 7:13, 14. Daniel beheld Christ borne in before the Father by the angels of God as our
Advocate in the judgment. E. W. 55; G. C.
480.

1 Tim. 2:5. There is *one* mediator between God
and men, the man Christ Jesus. G. C. 482.

Dan. 7:9, 10. God the Father sits as judge, the angels are witnesses, the books with their record
of every thought and intent of the heart, as
well as of every word and action, represent
the individual to be judged. Christ is the
mediator.

Acts 3:19-21. The sins of all *who have repented
of their sins will* be blotted out, thus cleansing
the heavenly sanctuary of all the sins of the
righteous. P. P. 357, 358.

Dan. 8:14. Daniel was shown that the sanctuary
would be cleansed at the end of the 2300 days,
or in the autumn of 1844.

Day of Atonement

Lev. 16:29, 30. On the tenth day of the seventh
Jewish year, the confessed sins of the righteous were cleansed from the sanctuary.

Isa. 59:2. Sin separates God from His people. P. K.
323.

Lev. 16:16, 33. Atonement means at-one-ment. The
atonement was for both apartments of the sanctuary and the people.

Lev. 16:7-19. Cleansed with blood.

Lev. 16:18, 19. Last work at the golden altar.
E. W. 280, 281.

Trans. has Azazel the "angel [strong one] who revolted." The oldest opinions of the Hebrews and Christians are that Azazel is the name of the devil.

Lev. 16:20-22. When the high priest had completed the work of atonement for the people, the sins were placed on Azazel.

Rev. 20:1-3. After every case is decided for eternity, Satan, the antitype, with the sins of the righteous placed upon him, is left on the desolate earth.

Lev. 16:23. High priest changed his garments.

Lev. 16:24-28. Clad in other garments, he proceeded to cleanse the court. At the end of the day nothing but ashes remained of sin.

Matt. 13:40-42. At the end of the world, Christ will cleanse the earth, the antitypical court, from all sin. G. C. 673.

Rev. 19:14-16. When He comes to do that work, He wears kingly, not priestly, garments. E. W. 286, 36.

Isa. 63:1-4. They are garments of vengeance.

Mal. 4:1-3. When the antitypical day of atonement is complete, there is nothing but ashes remaining of sin and sinners. E. W. 295.

Isa. 65:17, 18. Every trace of sin will be wiped from the face of the earth.

Peace-Offering

John 14:27. Christ left His peace on earth. D. A. 672.

John 16:33. Peace in tribulation. D. A. 335.

Lev. 3:1, 2, 8. Confessed sin over offering.

Isa. 57:21. No peace with a sinful heart. D. A. 336, 337.

Lev. 3:3-5; 7:30. The one desiring peace separated the fat.

Ps. 37:20. Fat represented sin.

2 Cor. 13:5. Must examine our hearts if we desire peace. D. A. 304, 305.

Lev. 7:32, 33. Shoulder given to the priest that offered the blood.

1 John 1:7. Christ's blood cleanses us.

Isa. 9:6. Government of all that concerns us must be laid on the shoulder of the Prince of Peace. D. A. 330, 331.

Isa. 22:22. The key to every path before us must be laid on Christ's shoulder.

Lev. 7:30, 31. Breast given the priest.

Isa. 40:11. Carries the lambs in His bosom.

John 13:23-25. John leaned on Christ's breast. Perfect open communion between the soul and Christ. A. A. 85, 86.

Deut. 18:3. Maw, or stomach, given priest.

Num. 11:4-10. No peace with appetite uncontrolled. P. P. 377, 378.

1 Cor. 10:6; Dan. 1:8. Peace with controlled appetite. P. K. 482, 483.

Deut. 18:3. Cheeks given priest.

of Him in peace."

The Altar of Incense

Ex. 30:1-6. Golden altar before the vail.

Ex. 30:7, 8. Perpetual incense renewed morning and evening. The high priest was to offer the incense.

Ex. 30:34-38. Special incense which could not be used for any other purpose.

Ex. 30:9. No strange incense could be offered.

Heb. 8:5. A shadow of heavenly service.

Rev. 8:2-5. John saw the heavenly altar.

Rev. 8:3. An angel officiated.

Jude 9; 1 Thess. 4:16; John 5:28, 29. Michael, the archangel, is Christ, our High Priest.

Rev. 8:3, 4, margin. Incense is added to the prayers. P. P. 359.

John 14:13, 14. The name, or righteous character, of Christ makes our prayers acceptable. T., v. 4, pp. 124, 528.

1 John 1:9; Isa. 61:10. Pardoned one clothed with righteousness. T., v. 4, p. 124.

Isa. 64:6. Our righteousness is strange incense.

Ex. 30:7, 8; Heb. 9:6. Incense was perpetual; hence, offered on day of atonement.

Rev. 8:3. Incense added to the prayers of *all* saints.

Rev. 5:8, margin. All prayers not answered at once. After they are accepted by the incense being added, they are put in golden vials to be answered in God's own time.

The First Angel's Message Announcing the Hour of God's Judgment

Rev. 14:6. The angel having the everlasting gospel is the first of a series of three angels. L. S. 278.

Rev. 14:7. The burden of the message is the hour of God's "judgment *is come*." Men are to fear God and give glory to Him. G. C. 355, 356.

Acts 24:25. This message could not have been given in Paul's day, for the judgment was then future.

2 Tim. 4:1. The day of judgment is connected with the coming of Christ.

Luke 21:36; 20:35. The righteous are "accounted worthy" before Christ comes.

Rev. 22:12. Christ brings His reward with Him.

Rev. 10:1-10. This message is based upon the contents of a "little book," which announces that time should be no longer.

Rev. 10:11. As this is followed by another worldwide message, it is not real time, but prophetic time, that ends.

Dan. 8:14. Daniel is the only "little book" that gives the 2300 days,—the longest prophetic period in the Bible, which ended in 1844.

Rev. 10:1-3. The proclamation of this message is compared to the roar of a lion.

Europe; while Wm. Miller and his co-laborers declared the message in America. G. C. 357-370.

Zech. 9:9; Luke 19:35-40. The disciples fulfilled prophecy at the time of Christ's triumphal entry into Jerusalem, but were disappointed. G. C. 351.

Rev. 10:8-10. In like manner God's people fulfilled prophecy during the ten years prior to 1844. As they studied the prophetic symbols in Daniel, the thought of Christ coming in 1844 was sweet to them, but the disappointment was bitter. G. C. 373.

Heb. 10:32-34. God desires that this experience should be kept in remembrance by His people.

Dan. 7:9, 10. The people expected the judgment to take place on earth and were disappointed in the location of the judgment and not the event.

It was by God's appointment that while heaven was interested in the opening of the judgment in heaven, Christ's followers on earth should have their love and thoughts all centered on the movements of their Saviour. G. C. 374, 457.

Second Angel's Message

Heb. 10:32-34. Many rejected the first angel's message and persecuted those who accepted it. G. C. 380.

Rev. 14:8. The second angel followed, announcing the fall of Babylon.

Rev. 17:5, 6. Babylon is the power that put to death the martyrs of Jesus.

Rev. 17:5, 18. Babylon represents an apostate church.

Rev. 17:5. The term Babylon includes mother and daughters. G. C. 382, 383.

Gen. 11:7, 9, margin. Babylon means confusion. G. C. 381.

Rev. 14:8. Lest any should doubt that Babylon is fallen, it is repeated twice. Gen. 41:32. The daughters as well as the mother are fallen.

Rev. 18:1-5. The message repeated with greater force. G. C. 603, 604.

Rev. 18:1. Great power attends the giving of the message.

Rev. 18:2. It is given when the "daughter churches" have become wholly corrupt.

Rev. 18:3. Unlawful connection with the nations the crowning sin.

2 Cor. 11:2; Eph. 5:23. Christ is the head of the church. When the churches appeal to the earthly governments to make religious laws, they are committing fornication and are unfaithful to their true husband, Christ. G. C. 381.

Rev. 17:3, 6. The mother church is represented as guiding the civil power, and being drunk with the blood of martyrs. G. C. 382.

Rev. 18:3. This union of church and state to be world-wide. G. C. 389, 390.

Rev. 18:4. God calls His people out of Babylon;

sages and is world-wide. Is addressed to "any man"; none are excluded. It is a warning against the worship of the beast and its image. G. C. 611.

Rev. 13:5-7. The beast is the power that persecuted the saints for 42 months, or 1260 years.

Dan. 7:25. The power that persecuted the people of God for 1260 years thinks to change the law of God. One power has arisen that claims to change the law of God. We quote from their own writings as follows:

"Q. What are the days which the church commands to be kept holy? . . .

"A. First the Sunday, or Lord's day, which we observe by apostolic example instead of the Sabbath. . . .

"Q. What warrant have you for keeping Sunday preferably to the ancient Sabbath which was Saturday?

"A. We have for it *the authority of the Catholic church* and apostolic *tradition.* . . ." Catholic Christian Instructed. chap., 23, p. 272.

Ex. 20:8-11. The law of God commands us to keep the seventh day, or Saturday, holy.

1 Sam. 15:22. Obedience highest type of worship. Gen. 22:5.

1 Kings 18:21. As in Elijah's day, all are asked

to decide whom they will serve. Joshua 24:15; G. C. 604.

Rev. 13:8. Only those whose names are in the book of life refuse to worship the beast.

Rev. 14:10. Those who obey the beast receive his mark and drink the unmixed wrath of God.

Rev. 15:1, 7. The unmixed wrath of God is the seven last plagues.

Rev. 14:9, 10. The seven last plagues are poured out on those who worship the beast and his image and receive his mark.

Eze. 9:1-11. Ezekiel describes this work.

Ps. 91:1-10. The righteous are shielded.

Rev. 3:10. Shielded because they have kept the word of God's patience.

Rev. 14:12. Finally only two parties, commandment-keepers and commandment-breakers. G. C. 605.

Rev. 14:14-16. When finished Christ gathers the harvest of the earth.

Rev. 22:14. All who have kept the commandments of God will have a right to the tree of life.

PASSOVER

"The Passover was to be both commemorative and typical, not only pointing back to the deliverance from Egypt, but forward to the greater deliverance which Christ was to accomplish in freeing His people from the bondage of sin." P. P. 277.

Type

Lev. 23:5. There was only one day in the year upon which the Passover could be kept. P. P. 539.

Ex. 12:6, ~~~~~ "between the two
evenings," or the middle of the afternoon.

Ex. 12:22. Blood on sides and top of the door-
frame.

Ex. 12:8, 9. The lamb roasted.

Ex. 12:8-10. Eaten *that night*. If any remained until morning, it was burned.

Ex. 12:11. Ready for marching while eating.

Ex. 12:8. Unleavened bread and bitter herbs eaten
with the flesh.

Ex. 12:29. While they were eating the destroying
angel passed over.

Ex. 12:4. Neighboring families were gathered together at this feast.

Ex. 12:48, 49. Strangers that complied with the
requirements could eat it.

Ex. 12:26, 27. The children were taught the meaning of the Passover.

Antitype

1 Cor. 5:7. Christ is our "Passover Lamb." G. C.
399.

John 11:47-54. The 10th day of the first month,
(31 A. D.) the council set Him apart for death.

John 18:28. Friday morning Jews had not eaten
the Passover.

John 19:14. Christ was crucified at the time of "the preparation of the Passover."

Matt. 27:46-50. Christ died between the evenings, about three o'clock, at the time the Passover lambs were being slain. D. A. 756.

John 19:31. The day following the crucifixion was an "high day"; that is, the yearly Passover Sabbath, and also the Sabbath of the Lord, the seventh day of the week.

Luke 23:54-56; Lev. 23:5-7. While Christ, the true Passover, rested in the tomb from His finished earthly work on the Passover Sabbath, the 15th day of the first month, His followers were resting according to the commandment, upon the same day, the creation Sabbath. The day from that time was doubly blessed. D. A. 769.

1 Cor. 15:20. Christ, the "first-fruits of them that slept." D. A. 785.

Matt. 27:52, 53. "Many bodies of the saints which slept arose" and followed Christ from the tomb.

Rom. 8:29. He was the "first-born among *many* brethren."

Eph. 4:7, 8, margin. When He ascended to heaven He took His company with Him as a sample of the final great harvest.

Lev. 23:10, 11, margin. In the type the priest waved a "handful," or sheaf, of the heads of the ripened grain before the Lord on the 16th day of the first month. D. A. 77, 786.

John 20:16, 17. In the early morning of that memorable 16th day of the first month, the Saviour had not ascended.

a symbol of ...
established and conducted in accordance with ...
plan, are among His most effective agencies for the
formation of Christian character and for the ad-
vancement of His work." T., v. 6, p. 430.

Duty of Husband

Gen. 2:24. Leave father and mother for wife.

Deut. 13:6-8. Husband should never allow his wife
to turn him from God.

Deut. 24:5. First year of married life, husband
should remain at home and *"cheer* up his
wife."

Prov. 5:18. Rejoice with his wife.

Eccl. 9:9. Live joyfully with her. M. H. 374,
375.

Eph. 5:25-33. "Love your wives, even as Christ
also loved the church and gave Himself for
it." M. H. 360.

Col. 3:19. Be not bitter against them.

Prov. 31:28. Commend and praise.

1 Peter 3:7. Honor the wife. T., v. 5, pp. 180,
181; M. H. 373, 374.

Mal. 2:14, 15. God is witness if any deal treach-
erously with their wives.

Matt. 19:3-9. One reason for separation.

1 Cor. 7:12-16. Convert wife by godly life.

The man who lives up to God's requirements will have a happy home. He can kneel with his wife and together their prayers will ascend unhindered to the throne of grace.

Duty of Wife

Gen. 3:6, 17-24. The wife should never, like Eve, ask her husband to disobey God. M. H. 361.

Prov. 12:4. A virtuous woman is a crown to her husband.

Eph. 5:23. Husband the head of the wife.

Eph. 5:33. Wife reverence the husband.

Titus 2:4, 5. Love and obey the husband.

Col. 3:18. "Wives, submit yourselves unto your own husbands *as it is fit in the Lord.*" If a husband commands a wife to disobey God, then obedience could not be *fit in the Lord.*

Prov. 19:13; 21:9, margin. A contentious wife makes an unhappy home.

Prov. 21:19, margin. Better dwell in the desert than with such a woman.

Prov. 31:10-12, 26. A husband can safely trust a virtuous woman who speaks kindly.

1 Cor. 7:10, 11. "Let not the wife depart from her husband."

Rom. 7:2, 3. The wife bound to her husband as long as he lives.

Mark 10:12. If the wife leaves her husband and marries another, she commits adultery.

1 Cor. 7:13, 16. Godly life may win unbelieving husband.

Titus 2:4. Love them. T., v. 2, p. 80.

Matt. 19:13, 14. Bring to Christ. T., v. 4, pp. 115, 199, 200.

Prov. 22:6; Eph. 6:4. Train for God. M. H. 44.

Deut. 4:9 Isa. 38:19. Instruct in God's word. E. 185.

Joel 1:3. Tell of God's judgments. E. 34, 35.

Ex. 10:2; Ps. 78:4. Of God's work. E. 52.

Deut. 32:46. Command them to obey God.

Gen. 48:15. Bless them.

Ps. 103:13. Pity them. T., v. 2, p. 57.

Job 42:15; 2 Cor. 12:14; 1 Tim. 5:8. Provide for them. T., v. 2, p. 85.

1 Tim. 3:4, 12. Rule them.

Prov. 13:24; 19:18; 23:13; 29:17; Heb. 12:7. Correct them.

Eph. 6:4; Col. 3:21. Do not provoke them.

Gen. 24:1-4; 28:1, 2. Not to make unholy connections for them.

Parental Control

Ps. 127:3. "Children are an heritage of the Lord."

Ex. 2:9. God offers wages to every parent just as surely as Pharaoh's daughter did to the mother of Moses.

Prov. 29:17; 10:1. Rest and delight of soul paid the faithful parent. T., v. 7, p. 186.

Prov. 29:15; 17:25; 15:20. Shame, contempt and bitterness, are the wages of the parents that fail to properly train their children. T., v. 7, p. 66.

Prov. 29:15; 22:15. No child naturally good.

1 Sam. 3:11-14. Restrain the child. T., v. 5, pp. 44, 45.

Prov. 31:26-28. Govern by law of kindness. T., v. 7, pp. 47, 48.

Prov. 19:18. Do not wait until it is too late to control the child.

Prov. 20:11. Every child reveals its character.

Prov. 23:13, 14. Do not withhold correction.

Prov. 13:24. True love will control. T., v. 5, pp. 319, 320.

Prov. 29:22. To strike a child in anger stirs up strife.

Prov. 25:28. Without self-control no one can properly train others. M. H. 131; P. P. 142, 143.

Prov. 16:32. Self-control of great value. M. H. 371, 372.

Result of Wrong Training

1 Sam. 2:27-34. The priesthood was taken from the family of Eli because he failed to control his children.

1 Sam. 2:23-25. Eli reproved his sons for their wrong course; but reproof alone is not sufficient.

1 Sam. 3:13. Parents must "restrain" and con-

1 Sam. 8:... ...
caused the office of ju... ...
uel's family.

2 Kings 19:37. Uncontrolled children will even slay their parents.

Prov. 17:25. A "foolish son" brings grief and bitterness to parents.

Result of Good Training

1 Sam. 3:19. The Lord is with good children. P. K. 245, 246.

2 Tim. 3:15. They are acquainted with the Scriptures.

Prov. 28:7. A wise son obeys the law of God.

Col. 3:20. God is well pleased with obedient children.

Acts 2:39. They share in the promises of God.

Eph. 6:2. A blessing is pronounced upon good children.

Gen. 46:29. A good son will never be ashamed to love and caress his parents.

Prov. 13:1. A wise son will heed the instruction of his parents.

Prov. 23:22. Parents in old age will be treated with respect by good children.

Job 32:6, 7. One of judgment will recognize age and experience.

3

Heb. 12:9. The respect and reverence paid to earthly parents is a reminder of the reverence due the Lord.

Home Influences

Ps. 101:7. Deceitful and wicked people should not be kept in the house.

1 Cor. 15:33. You can not keep evil people in your family without their exerting an evil influence over your children. T., v. 4, pp. 110-112.

1 Cor. 5:6. A little leaven leaveneth the whole lump.

Eph. 6:4. Parents should not provoke their children.

Col. 3:21. Should not discourage them.

Prov. 22:6. Children should be trained.

1 Tim. 3:4, 5. One that does not control his own family can not be trusted to manage the things of God.

Titus 1:6, 7. The children of a bishop should be above reproach.

1 Tim. 3:12. A deacon should control his family.

Gen. 18:17-19. God can trust a man that commands his children and his household. E. 187.

2 Cor. 12:14. Parents should provide for their children.

1 Tim. 5:8. Every Christian should supply the needs of his family.

Education in the Homes

Deut. 6:7-9. Teach diligently. The word of God should be the topic of daily conversation in the home and out of it. P. P. 141.

Deut. 4:9-13. Teach the children about the giving of the law.

are properly taught.

Esther 2:20. Children properly educated will obey their parents after they are grown.

Gen. 45:7, 8. Children, educated after God's plan, can be sent as foreign missionaries at an early age. P. P. 244.

Joshua 4:6, 7. Children should be taught by the objects around them. P. P. 572.

Ex. 12:25-27. Taught by object-lessons. E. 186.

Ex. 13:8. Taught by customs.

1 Tim. 1:4. Fictitious reading should be discarded. T., v. 2, p. 410.

1 Tim. 4:7. Refuse profane writing. E. 227.

1 Tim. 6:20. Shun science, falsely so called.

Deut. 11:19-21. Teaching the word of God in the home as God directs, will make the home "as the days of heaven upon earth."

The Fifth Commandment

Ex. 20:12. The new earth promised to the one who honors his parents.

Lev. 19:3. Not only in childhood should children honor their parents, but after they are men they are to honor "mother and father." T., v. 3, p. 294.

Gen. 9:20-27. Disrespect shown to even a drunken

parent brings punishment, and respect brings reward.

Ex. 21:15. In olden times it was a serious offense to smite a parent.

Ex. 21:17. Cursing a parent was punishable with death.

Deut. 27:16. A curse was pronounced upon the child that "setteth light by his parents."

Deut. 21:18-21. The stubborn and rebellious children were punished by death.

Jer. 35:18, 19. Respect and obedience rewarded.

Mark 7:9-13. Any attempt to evade providing for parents is a violation of the commandments of God.

Matt. 15:5-7. One who claims to be a Christian and neglects to care for his parents is a hypocrite.

Col. 3:20. Obedience is well pleasing.

Eph. 6:1. All obedience must be according to the word of God. *Obey in the Lord.*

Matt. 10:37. While children should respect parents, whether they are good or bad, we must love and obey God above all parents.

Lev. 19:32. Age commands respect.

PRAYER

Prayer is the link that connects us with Christ; or, as it is sometimes stated, "Prayer is the key that opens heaven." Few realize the mighty power there is in the prayer of faith.

"The prayer of the humble suppliant Christ presents as His own desire in that soul's behalf. Every sincere prayer is heard in heaven. It may not be

Heb. 11:6. "He that cometh to God must believe that He is, and that He is a rewarder of them that diligently seek Him." D. A. 200.

Matt. 6:12-15. We must forgive those that have wronged us as we wish God to forgive us.

Matt. 5:23-25. If others have anything against us, we should seek to make it right.

Ps. 66:18. There should be a hatred of sin. God hears prayer when the sinner is ready to exchange sin for righteousness.

Prov. 28:9. There must be an obedient mind. The transgressor of the law is heard if he is willing to obey. T., v. 9, p. 164.

John 15:16. Our requests must be presented in the name of Jesus. D. A. 668.

Job 35:13. Pride and vanity should be put away.

Jas. 1:6, 7. The individual that one day asks God to help him overcome sin and the next day chooses sin, can not expect help.

Answered Prayer

Rom. 8:26, 27. "The spirit itself maketh intercession for us with groanings which cannot be uttered."

Dan. 9:21-23. Prayers are sometimes answered immediately.

Luke 18:2-7. Sometimes after delay. C. O. L. 142, 143.

2 Cor. 12:8, 9. As earthly parents who really love their children will give them what is best rather than what they cry for, so God sometimes answers our prayers different from our desires.

Jer. 33:3; Eph. 3:20. God often gives us far more than we ever think of asking for.

Jas. 5:14-16. The sick will be healed in answer to the prayer of faith.

1 John 5:14. All requests are to be according to God's will. M. H. 229.

1 John 3:22. The one who obeys God can expect answers to his prayers.

Phil. 4:6. With thanksgiving let your requests be made known unto God.

Col. 4:2. "Continue in prayer, and watch in the same with thanksgiving."

Matt. 21:22; Jas. 1:6. Prayer is carried on the wings of faith. D. A. 126.

2 Chron. 30:27. Prayers of faith enter God's holy dwelling place in heaven. A. A. 564.

Acts 12:5-11. Angels are sent to answer the prayers of God's people. C. O. L. 341, 342.

Secret Prayer

Matt. 6:6. If we grow in grace, we must have seasons of secret communion with the Lord. T., v. 6, pp. 47, 50; v. 5, p. 161.

Mark 1:35. If the day is crowded with cares, we can do as the Saviour did,—arise before daylight in the morning and spend the time alone with God.

1 Thess. 5:17. We should be in a prayerful frame of mind continually. T., v. 5, pp. 200, 201.

Job 22:27, 28. It is the privilege of the Christian to believe that his prayer is heard.

Isa. 43:26. The Lord is pleased when we plead the promises He has made.

Isa. 41:21. God invites us to produce our cause, and bring forth our strong reasons.

Luke 11:1. We should ask the Lord to teach us how to pray.

Rom. 8:26, 27. The Holy Spirit presents the prayer of the broken and contrite heart before God in an acceptable manner.

Amos 5:4. There is life in earnest prayer. T., v. 6, p. 266; G. C. 621, 622.

Phil. 4:6. We should always thank the Lord for what He has done for us when we present our requests for greater blessings. T., v. 5, p. 317.

Family Prayer

Matt. 18:19. The Lord's word is pledged to answer the united prayer of two or more individuals.

Matt. 18:20. As the family of two or more kneel in prayer, it is their privilege to claim the promise of God's presence with them. T., v. 6, p. 357.

Acts 2:46, 47. A church whose members have daily prayer in their homes will always be a growing church.

Gen. 12:7, 8. Abraham erected a family altar wherever he lived.

Gen. 35:2-4. Jacob gathered his family together for family worship.

Gen. 35:5. A family that is faithful in worship will be respected by their neighbors.

Joshua 24:15. Every Christian should say with Joshua, "As for me and my house, we will serve the Lord."

Job 1:5. Job made offerings for his family continually.

Jer. 10:25. The families that do not have family worship are classed with the heathen. M. H. 392, 393.

Jer. 10:25. The cause of God is "devoured," "consumed," and made "desolate" by families that do not honor God sufficiently to have family worship.

For Whom Should We Pray?

Kings and all in authority, 1 Tim. 2:2. Ministers, 2 Cor. 1:11; Phil. 1:19. The church, Ps. 122:6; Isa. 62:6, 7. All saints, Eph. 6:18. All men, 1 Tim. 2:1. Children, Gen. 17:18; Matt. 15:22. Masters, Gen. 24:12-14. Servants, Luke 7:2, 3. Friends, Job 42:8, 10. Fellow-countrymen, Rom. 10:1. The sick, Jas. 5:14; T., v. 5, pp. 315, 443. Persecutor, Matt. 5:44. Enemies among whom we

prayed."

Acts 20:36. Paul "kneeled down and prayed."

2 Chron. 6:13. Solomon "kneeled down upon his knees before all the congregation" and prayed.

Matt. 26:39. The Saviour when in agony "fell on His face, and prayed."

1 Chron. 21:16. David when in distress fell upon his face in prayer. G. C. 156, 157.

Joshua 5:14. Joshua fell upon his face and worshiped.

Num. 16:20-22. Moses and Aaron fell upon their faces and prayed.

Mark 11:25. One may stand while praying.

Isa. 38:1, 2. Hezekiah prayed while lying in bed.

Isa. 1:15. Some spread forth their hands while praying.

Ps. 28:2. The psalmist lifted up his hands toward the heavenly sanctuary when he prayed.

Lam. 2:19. Whatever the posture, the heart must be poured out before God.

Ps. 66:18. "If I regard iniquity in my heart, the Lord will not hear me."

Prov. 28:9. "He that turneth away his ear from hearing the law, even his prayer shall be an abomination."

When prayer delights the least, then learn to say,
"Soul, now is greatest need that thou shouldst
pray."

THE BIBLE SABBATH

"Hallowed by the Creator's rest and blessing,
the Sabbath was kept by Adam in his innocence
in holy Eden; by Adam, fallen, yet repentant, when
he was driven from his happy estate. It was kept
by all the patriarchs, from Abel to righteous Noah,
to Abraham, to Jacob. When the chosen people
were in bondage in Egypt, many, in the midst of
prevailing idolatry, lost their knowledge of God's
law; but when the Lord delivered Israel, He proclaimed His law in awful grandeur to the as-
sembled multitude, that they might know His will,
and fear and obey Him forever. From that day
to the present, the knowledge of God's law has
been preserved in the earth, and the Sabbath of
the fourth commandment has been kept." G. C.
453.

The Sabbath

"The Sabbath is a golden clasp that unites God
and His people." T., v. 6, p. 351.

Gen. 2:3. Instituted by God.

Gen. 2:2, 3; Ex. 20:11. The Sabbath is a memorial of creation. E. 251.

Ex. 20:9-11. The seventh day is the Sabbath of
the Bible.

Mark 2:27. It was made for man.

Gen. 2:3. God blessed the Sabbath.

Ex. 31:15. Sanctified the Sabbath.

Ex. 20:11. Hallowed the Sabbath.

orated in the

Neh. 9:12-14. The Lord shows favor to His people in appointing a Sabbath.

Ex. 23:12. Considerate kindness was shown in appointing the Sabbath.

Ex. 31:13. The Sabbath is a sign of God's power to sanctify His people.

Heb. 4:4, 9. The Sabbath is a type of the heavenly rest.

Christ and the Sabbath

Mark 2:28. Christ is Lord of the Sabbath. D. A. 288.

Luke 4:16. Jesus was accustomed to keep the Sabbath when He was on the earth.

Matt. 24:20. Taught His disciples to pray that they might not break the Sabbath. D. A. 630.

Luke 4:31; 6:6. Christ taught on the Sabbath day.

John 5:5-9. Healed on the Sabbath day.

Mark 3:1-5. He taught that it was right to perform acts of mercy on the Sabbath day. D. A. 286.

Matt. 12:12; Luke 13:16. The Saviour recognized the Sabbath law.

Ex. 20:10; Deut. 5:14. Servants and cattle should be allowed to rest upon the Sabbath.

Lev. 23:3; Ex. 20:10. No manner of work is to be done on the Sabbath. T., v. 6, pp. 354-356.

Neh. 10:31; 13:15-17. No purchases are to be made. P. K. 667, 671.

Neh. 13:19; Jer. 17:21. No burdens are to be carried. P. K. 411.

Ex. 16:23. Food prepared the day before. T., v. 6, p. 357; M. H. 307.

Gen. 1:5, 8, 13, 19, 23, 31. Day begins with the evening.

Lev. 23:32; Mark 1:21, 32. Sabbath begins at sunset.

Neh. 13:19. All work set aside when it *begins to be dark, before the Sabbath*.

Acts 16:13. Divine worship is to be celebrated on the Sabbath.

Acts 13:27; 15:21. The Scriptures are to be read on the Sabbath.

Acts 13:14, 15, 42-44; 17:2; 18:4. The word of God is to be preached on the Sabbath. A. A. 229.

Num. 28:9; Matt. 12:5; John 7:23. Work connected with religious services is allowed on the Sabbath.

Matt. 12:1; Luke 13:15, 16; 14:1. Necessary wants may be supplied on the Sabbath day.

The Relation of God and His People to the Sabbath

Ex. 20:10; Lev. 23:3; Deut. 5:14. It is the Sabbath of the Lord thy God.

Ex. 31:15. The Sabbath of rest. P. P. 47.

Ex. 16:23. The rest of the holy Sabbath.

balances and short m̲e̲a̲s̲u̲r̲e̲.

Neh. 13:22. Saints observe the Sabbath.

Ps. 118:24; 58:13. Saints rejoice in the Sabbath.

Neh. 13:15, 20, 21. Testify against those who desecrate the Sabbath.

Isa. 58:13, 14. There is a blessedness in honoring it. D. A. 207.

Isa. 56:2-6. There is a blessing in keeping the Sabbath. P. P. 48.

Isa. 66:22, 23. The Sabbath will be kept throughout eternity.

The Wicked and the Sabbath

Lam. 1:7. The wicked mock at the Sabbath.

Isa. 56:2. They pollute it.

Neh. 13:17. They profane it. P. P. 113.

Amos 8:5-7. The wicked weary of the Sabbath.

Eze 22:26. They hide their eyes from the Sabbath.

Neh. 13:15. They also bear burdens upon the Sabbath.

Neh. 10:31. The wicked traffic on the Sabbath.

Luke 13:14; John 9:16. Sometimes they pretend to be zealous for it.

The First Day of the Week

There are nine references in the Bible to the first day of the week, as follows: Gen. 1:5; Matt. 28:1; Mark 16:1, 2, 9; Luke 24:1; John 20:1; 20:19; Acts 20:7; 1 Cor. 16:2.

The first day of the week was named by Jehovah 6,000 years ago. The six inspired writers that mention it, call it by the same name,—the first day of the week. None allude to it as the holy rest day, while three of them state it came the *day after the Sabbath,* showing that they did not regard it as the Sabbath. P. K. 183, 184.

It is classed among the working days. Eze. 46:1. Paul bore the following testimony 32 years this side of the cross: "I have committed nothing against the people or *customs of our fathers.*" Acts 28:17. If he had kept any other Sabbath than the seventh-day Sabbath, he would have departed from the customs of his fathers.

The Weekly Cycle

Gen. 1:5, 8, 13, 19, 23, 31; Gen. 2:1-3. The weekly cycle made at creation. Days numbered, but not named. P. P. 111.

Gen. 4:3, margin. They gathered for worship at the close of the cycle of days.

Eze. 46:1. Six of the days are called working days; the remaining one is a rest day.

Gen. 2:2, 3. All are alike except the seventh day, which was blessed and sanctified.

Isa. 58:13. God calls it His "holy day."

Ex. 20:8-11. It is called the "Sabbath of the Lord thy God."

Mark 2:28. "The Son of man is Lord also of the Sabbath."

The week, unlike the day, month, and year, is not connected with the movements of any heavenly bodies. The names of the seven days of which the week is composed were derived by the Egyptians from the seven celestial bodies then known. The Romans, in their names for the days, observed the same order, distinguishing them as follows:—

Dies Solis,	Sun's day,	Sunday
Dies Lunae,	Moon's day,	Monday
Dies Martis,	Mars' day,	Tuesday
Dies Mercurii,	Mercury's day.	Wednesday
Dies Jovis,	Jupiter's day,	Thursday
Dies Veneris,	Venus' day,	Friday
Dies Saturni,	Saturn's day,	Saturday

We can see at a glance the origin of our English names for the first, second and seventh days; the remaining four are named from Tiu, Woden, Thor, and Frigga, northern deities equivalent to Mars, Mercury, Jupiter, and Venus, in classical mythology.

Isa. 66:22, 23. The weekly cycle will continue on the new earth, and all will gather for worship upon the Sabbath.

Ceremonial Sabbaths

Lev. 23:7, 8, 21, 24, 25, 27, 32, 39. There are seven ceremonial Sabbaths as follows:—

1. 15th of Abib; 2. 23rd of Abib; 3. Pentecost;

4. 1st of the 7th month; 5. 10th of the 7th month; 6. 15th of the 7th month; 7. 22nd of the 7th month. These were annual Sabbaths, coming only once a year. As they always came on the same day of the month, they would come only occasionally on the 7th day of the week.

Col. 2:16, 17. These Sabbaths were all shadows of things to come.

Heb. 9:8-11. The types, or shadowy service, ceased at the cross. D. A. 774.

Matt. 27:50, 51. At the death of Christ God rent the vail of the temple, thus showing that the shadowy service had ended.

Heb. 9:10; Rom. 14:1-6; Col. 2:16. All of these ceremonial Sabbaths were connected with the annual feast days. On the Passover Sabbath bitter herbs were mingled with the feast. The day of atonement was a fast day; the others were feast days.

Lev. 23:38. These annual Sabbaths were separate and distinct from the Sabbath of the Lord.

Ex. 20:10. The seventh day of the week is the Sabbath of the Lord.

Ex. 20:8-11. "Meats and drinks" not connected with the weekly Sabbath.

Ex. 20:11. Seventh-day Sabbath a memorial of creation. D. A. 289.

Isa. 66:22, 23. As long as the world stands the memorial of creation will be celebrated.

day. D. A. 204, 211.

John 9:14-16. They thought He was not of God because He healed on the Sabbath day. D. A. 471, 472.

Matt. 12:10-12. The Saviour referred them to the Scriptures, stating that it was *lawful* to do acts of mercy on the Sabbath day, thus recognizing the Sabbath law. D. A. 285.

John 15:10. Jesus repudiated every charge of breaking the Sabbath by declaring that He kept His Father's commandments.

Mark 7:6-12. He refused to honor "tradition of men," substituted for God's law.

Isa. 42:21. The prophet Isaiah, looking down through the ages to the time of Christ, said that He would "magnify the law and make it honorable."

Luke 4:16. Jesus kept the Sabbath.

Matt. 24:20. He taught His disciples to honor it.

Luke 23:54-56. His followers kept it; Jesus never changed the Sabbath.

Did the Disciples Change the Sabbath?

Gen. 2:2, 3. It was the *seventh day* of the week that was first sanctified and set apart as the Sabbath of the Lord.

Ex. 20:8-11. It was the *same* seventh day that the followers of the Saviour kept while He lay dead in Joseph's new tomb. Luke 23:54-56.

Mark 16:1, 2. The Sabbath of the New Testament comes on the day before the first day of the week.

Luke 23:54-56; 24:1. From these verses we see that the Sabbath of the New Testament was the day between Friday, the preparation day, and Sunday, the first day of the week.

Acts 13:14, 15, 42-44. Paul preached in Ephesus on the Sabbath day.

Acts 16:12, 13. Work in Philippi opened with the Sabbath service.

Acts 17:2. Thessalonica church had Sabbath service.

Acts 18:4, 11. For one and a half years Paul held Sabbath services in Corinth.

Acts 28:17. If the apostles had not kept the seventh-day Sabbath, Paul could not have said that they had done nothing against the customs of the Jews.

Acts 15:21. As late as the year 52 A. D., 21 years this side of the cross, in every city the Scriptures were "read in the synagogues *every* Sabbath day." This Sabbath day was the same day that had been kept from the days of Moses.

Acts 13:42, 44. The Jews and believing Gentiles kept the same day for the Sabbath. There is no mention in the New Testament of any change of the Sabbath to the first day of the week. The disciples did not change the Sabbath. G. C. 451; P. K. 372.

powerful that wherever it had so powerful the Sabbath, and exalted the first day of the week. This was a gradual work, taking several centuries for its accomplishment.

In the year A. D. 321, Constantine issued the following edict: "Let all the judges and townspeople, and the occupation of all trades rest on the venerable day of the sun; but let those who are situated in the country freely and at full liberty attend to the business of agriculture; because it often happens that no other day is so fit for sowing corn and planting vines; lest, the critical moment being let slip, men should lose the commodities granted by heaven." This is the first Sunday law. G. C. 53.

The church favored the keeping of Sunday, and different edicts were issued from time to time; but, notwithstanding all this, many Christians still kept the seventh-day Sabbath "according to the commandment."

Because the practise of keeping the seventh-day Sabbath was evidently gaining ground in the Eastern church, the following decree was passed in the council held in Laodicea (A. D. 364); "That members of the church should not rest from work on the Sabbath-day like the Jews, but should labor on that day, and preferring in honor the Lord's day; then, if it be in their power, should rest from work as Christians."—Sermons on the Sacrament and the Sabbath, pp. 122, 123. G. C. 65.

"In Augsburg Confession, which was drawn up by Melancthon (and approved by Luther), to the question, 'What ought we to think of the Lord's day?' it is answered that the Lord's day, Easter, Whitsuntide, and other such holy days, ought to be kept, *because they are appointed* by the church."

Dan. 7:25. There is no account in the Bible of any Sabbath of the Lord, except the seventh-day Sabbath; but Daniel prophesied of a power that would think to change the law of God. P. K. 179,

Eze. 22:26-28; 13:10-12. Ezekiel saw the law violated, Sabbath profaned, and those who should have led in right lines, using "untempered mortar," or giving falsehood instead of God's words. P. P. 477.

The following is taken from the "Catholic Christian Instructed," 17th edition, revised and corrected, pp. 272, 273:—

"Ques. What warrant have you for keeping Sunday preferably to the ancient Sabbath which was Saturday?

"Ans. We have for it the authority of the Catholic church, and apostolic tradition.

"Ques. Does the Scripture anywhere command the Sunday to be kept for the Sabbath?

"Ans. The Scripture commands us to hear the church (St. Matt. 18:17; St. Luke 10:16), and to hold fast the traditions of the apostles. 2 Thess. 2:15. But the Scripture does not in particular mention this change of the Sabbath.

"St. John speaks of the Lord's day (Rev. 1:10); but he does not tell us what day of the week this was, much less does he tell us what day was to take the place of the Sabbath ordained in the commandments. St. Luke speaks of the disciples meeting together to break bread on the first day of

those who pretend to [illegible] Sunday, whilst they take no notice of other feasts ordained by the same church authority, show that they act more by humor, than by reason and religion; since Sundays and holidays all stand upon the same foundation, namely, the ordinance of the church."

"The "Doctrinal Catechism," pp. 174, 352, offers proof that Protestants are not guided by the Scriptures. We present two of the questions and answers:—

"Ques. Have you any other way of proving that the church has power to institute festivals of precept?

"Ans. Had she not such power, she could not have done that in which all modern religionists agree with her,—she could not have substituted the observance of Sunday, the first day of the week, for the observance of Saturday, the seventh day, a change for which there is no scriptural authority.

"Ques. When Protestants do profane work on Saturday, or the seventh day of the week, do they follow the Scriptures as their only rule of faith— do they find this permission clearly laid down in the Sacred Volume?

"Ans. On the contrary, they have only the authority of tradition for this practise. In profaning Saturday, they violate one of God's commandments, which He has never clearly abrogated,—'Remember that thou keep holy the Sabbath day.'" G. C. 447.

The Seal of God

Esther 8:8. A seal attached to a document makes it legal. A legal seal gives name of person issuing seal, also his title and territory. In this text Ahasuerus was the *name*, king the *title*, and Persia the *territory* over which he ruled.

Rom. 4:11. Sign and seal synonymous.

Isa. 8:16. The seal of earthly rulers is attached to their laws to make them binding upon their subjects. The seal of God is attached to His law to make it binding upon all His subjects. P. P. 307.

Matt. 5:17, 18; Rom. 7:7; Jas. 2:8-12; Ex. 24:12; Deut. 4:9-13. God's law is the ten commandments.

Ex. 20:8-11. Read carefully each commandment and find where God has attached His seal,—His name, title and territory.

Ex. 20:11. In the last part of the fourth commandment, we find all the specifications of the seal. Lord, His name; Creator, His title; His territory, the heavens and earth. All within that territory are amenable to His law.

Ex. 31:13. The Sabbath is a sign or seal of God's authority. G. C. 605.

Gen. 2:2, 3. There were three steps in making the Sabbath. 1. God rested on the seventh day; that made it God's rest day. 2. He blessed the seventh day after He had rested; that made all succeeding seventh-days God's blessed rest days. 3. He sanctified it, or set it apart for a holy use, and it became God's blessed, holy, rest day. D. A. 281.

Eze. 20:12. Just as the seventh day is set apart for a holy use, so the keeping of the Sabbath becomes a sign of sanctification between God and the individual that keeps it. In the act of keeping the Sabbath he acknowledges he is set apart for holy work. God is first in all his work and business. E. 250.

Ex. 20:8. The Sabbath is holy; God wishes us to regard it as holy time.

Ex. 31:13. The one that in the fear of God will keep the Sabbath holy, becomes holy.

Ex. 31:17. The rest, refreshing, and blessing were placed in the seventh day, not in any other day.

Num. 23:19, 20. The blessing can not be transferred by man to any other day. God's blessing can not be reversed by man.

1 Chron. 17:27. God's blessing continues forever.

Isa. 66:22, 23. The Sabbath will be God's blessed, holy, rest day throughout eternity.

The Sealing Work

Isa. 8:16, 17. The command was given to bind up the testimony and seal the law, at the time they were waiting for the coming of the Lord. The law was broken and needed binding up.

The seal had been taken from the law and must be replaced. P. K. 678.

Isa. 58:13. The prophet foretold a period when the Sabbath would be trampled under foot. The seal disregarded and taken from the law.

Rev. 7:1-4. John saw a special sealing message going to the earth.

Rev. 7:1. Winds denote war and strife. Dan. 11:40. The affairs of all earthy powers are held until the number of the redeemed is made up. The judgments of God that will affect the atmosphere, land, and water (Rev. 6:12-16), can not be poured out upon the earth until the sealing work is finished.

Rev. 7:1. When God said, "After these things," He must have referred to the events of Rev. 6:12, 13, as the last verses of Revelation 6 follow the sealing work. The stars fell in 1833. The special work of restoring the seal of God—the fourth commandment—to its proper position in the law of God, could not come earlier than that date.

Rev. 11:18, 19. In the time of the judgment of the dead, the temple of God was opened in heaven, and the ark containing the law revealed. After the disappointment of 1844, the people of God saw the light on the subject of the sanctuary in heaven. Then they saw the binding claim of the fourth commandment as well as the nine other commands of the decalogue. The Sabbath reform commenced at that time; by 1848 it began to be recognized as the fulfillment of Rev. 7:1-4.

Rev. 7:2. Like the sunlight on the earth,—first

The Hundred and Forty-four Thousand, or the Sealed Ones

Rev. 7:4. There are 144,000 of the sealed ones. Many children of God are dying daily who have never had their attention called to this truth, and are saved among the innumerable company. Rev. 7:9.

Eze. 9:1-4. The seal is here spoken of as a mark, which is the same as a sign.

Rev. 7:3. The seal is placed in the forehead,—the mind, or seat of affections.

Eze. 9:4. Those who have a burden of soul for others and are grieved on account of sin, will receive the mark. T., v. 7, p. 144.

Rev. 14:1. They receive the name of the Father.

Ex. 34:5, 6. The name of God is His character. Those who are sealed will partake of His character.

2 Tim. 2:19. All who have the seal depart from iniquity.

Rev. 14:3-5. They are to stand without fault, are to have no guile. They will follow the Lamb wheresoever He goeth. T., v. 5, pp. 214, 216.

Eph. 4:30; 1:13. The Holy Spirit places the seal.

Rev. 14:9-12. They refuse the mark of the beast and his image. P. K. 188.

Rev. 15:1-3. This company stands on Mount Zion triumphant over every foe. God, not man, does the numbering.

Num. 3:39; 26:62; Matt. 14:21; 15:38; Acts 19:7. The way God numbers.

Eze. 9:11, margin. When every one who will accept the message is sealed, the angel reports that the work is finished.

Eze. 9:5-7. The judgments of God follow the sealing work.

Eze. 9:8, 9. So many that had been counted with Israel were slain that it looked as if all the people of God would be destroyed.

Rom. 9:6. All who make a profession are not really Israel.

Eze. 9:6. Old and young stand on their own individual records.

Eze. 14:20. No one will be shielded or saved because of father's or mother's righteousness. Only an individual experience in the things of God will save any one.

The Law and the Gospel

The law is the gospel concealed:	The gospel is the law revealed.
The law is the gospel fullness delayed:	The gospel is the lawfulness portrayed.
The law is the gospel contained:	The gospel is the law maintained.
The law is the gospel sighted:	The gospel is the law lighted.
The law is Christ designed:	The gospel is Christ enshrined.

3rd commandment,—Matt. 5:33-37.

4th commandment,—Mark 2:27, 28; Matt. 24:20; 28:1; Mark 16:1, 2; Luke 4:16; 23:54-56.

5th commandment,—Matt. 15:4-9; Eph. 6:1-3.

6th commandment,—Matt. 5:21, 22; 1 John 3:15.

7th commandment,—Matt. 5:27, 28; 19:9, 18.

8th commandment,—Matt. 19:18; 15:19.

9th commandment,—Matt. 19:18.

10th commandment,—Rom. 7:7; Matt. 19:21, 22.

THE TWO COVENANTS

OLD COVENANT. Made when Israel came from Egypt, Heb. 8:9; Jer. 31:32. First promise to obey, Ex. 19:5-8. Second promise, Ex. 24:3. Third promise, Ex. 24:4-7. Covenant then ratified by blood, Ex. 24:8; Heb. 9:17-21. This is called the first covenant, *not because* it was the first one made, but because it was the first one ratified by blood, P. P. 371. This covenant was broken, Jer. 31:32. They promised to obey in their own strength and failed. Only in Christ's strength can any keep their covenant with God, P. P. 372.

NEW COVENANT. Law of God the basis, Jer. 31:33; Heb. 8:10. Forgiveness of sins in covenant, Jer. 31:34. Christ's blood only cleanses from sin, 1 John 1:7. Christ, a lamb slain from the foundation of the world, Rev. 13:8; therefore, the new covenant began in the beginning and extends until sin is destroyed forever, P. P. 370. Obedience to the law of God through the blood of Christ is the object of the everlasting, or new covenant, Heb. 13:20, 21. First promise of a Saviour, Gen. 3:15. The Lord pledged the new, or everlasting covenant, to Noah and his posterity, Gen. 9:9-17. The rainbow given as a pledge of the covenant, Gen. 9:13-16. Covenant pledged to Abraham and his children, Gen. 17:2-7, 21; P. P. 371. Abraham's seed, Gal. 3:16, 29. Covenant same as will, or last testament, Gal. 3:15, margin; Heb. 9:16, 17. Death of testator seals the will, or testament, Heb. 9:16. Christ's death sealed or ratified the new covenant, John 19:28-30.

Even a man's will can not be broken after the death of the testator, Gal. 3:15. Nothing can be added to Christ's covenant after His death; for that reason He instituted baptism and the Lord's supper,—memorial of His death and resurrection, *before* the events had taken place, that the memorials might become a part of the new covenant, John 4:1; Rom. 6:3-5; Matt. 26:26-28. Christ renewed the Sabbath commandment before His death, Matt. 24:20. The strongest advocates for Sunday observance give nothing earlier than the first day of the week upon which Christ arose from the dead as evidence for Sunday observance; but it is on

nant, P. P. 401.

sight, trusting in his own strength, lives under the old covenant. Under which covenant are you living?

THE LAW OF GOD

"Christ's death did not make the law of none effect; it did not slay the law, lessen its holy claims; nor did it detract from its sacred dignity. The death of Christ proclaimed the justice of His Father's law in punishing the transgressor, in that He consented to suffer the penalty of the law Himself, in order to save fallen man from its curse. The death of God's beloved Son on the cross, shows the immutability of the law of God. His death magnifies the law and makes it honirable, and gives evidence to man of its changeless character. . . . The death of Christ justified the claims of the law." T., v. 2, p. 201.

The Law of God before It Was Proclaimed upon Mount Sinai

Rom. 5:13. "Sin is not imputed where there is no law." T., v. 8, p. 207.

Gen. 2:17; 3:1-7. Eve coveted the fruit and then stole. P. P. 55, 56.

Gen. 4:7. Sin lay at Cain's door. P. P. 81-83.

Gen. 13:13; 19:4-11. Sodomites were "sinners before the Lord exceedingly."

Gen. 39:7-10. Sin to break 7th commandment. P. P. 217.

Gen. 9:20-27. Cursed for breaking the 5th commandment.

Ex. 16:22-30. Sabbath 30 days before Sinai.

Ex. 5:5. Israelites kept Sabbath. P. P. 258.

Gen. 35:2-5. Idolatry a sin.

Gen. 6:5, margin. The antediluvians broke *all* the law; for every imagination of the heart was *evil* every day. P. P. 159.

The Giving of the Law

Deut. 4:32, 33. Greatest event in history.

Ex. 19:1; Num. 1:45, 46. Audience of at least 1,000,000.

Ex. 19:10, 11. Three days' preparation.

Ex. 19:12, 13. Bounds around Sinai.

Ex. 19:16-20. Wonderful display of grandeur. T., v. 8, p. 198.

Ps. 68:8, 17; Heb. 12:26. Thousands of angels. Whole earth shook.

Deut. 4:12, 13; Ex. 20:1-17. From the midst of the glory God spoke the ten commandments. P. P. 303-311.

Deut. 5:22. God spoke no other words.

Deut. 4:9, 10. We should never forget that great display of power and glory. Teach the children about it. T., v. 6, p. 10.

Ex. 24:12. Moses called into the Mount.

Ex. 31:18. God gave unto Moses "two tables of

second table

The Law of God

Ps. 19:7. The law is perfect. G. C. 468.

Rom. 7:12. Holy, just, and good. G. C. 433, 434.

Matt. 5:17, 18. Christ forbade anyone even thinking that He would change the law.

Col. 1:25, margin. To fulfill is to preach fully.

Isa. 42:21. Christ magnified the law.

Matt. 5:21-26; 1 John 3:15. Hatred in heart breaks the law.

Ps. 119:96. The commandments are exceedingly broad.

Matt. 5:27, 28. Impure thoughts break the law. D. A. 310.

Matt. 5:33-37. The use of bywords is swearing.

Mark 7:7-13. Tradition can never take the place of the law.

Matt. 19:16-22. There is life in obedience.

Luke 10:25, 26. Carefully consider *"what is written in the law"*; take it as it reads.

John 15:10. Christ kept the law. T., v. 8, p. 208; C. O. L. 282, 283.

Matt 22:34-40. The law embraces our full duty to God and fellowmen. G. C. 467.

Matt. 12:1-8. Christ's disciples accused of breaking the Sabbath. He was Lord of it. D. A. 204, 284-286.

Matt. 12:10-14. "It is *lawful* to do well on the Sabbath-day."

Luke 4:16. Christ kept the 4th commandment.

1 Peter 2:21. Follow His steps.

Converting Power in the Law

Ps. 19:7. Converts the soul. D. A. 308.

Rom. 3:19; Num. 15:16. All the world subject to the law. T., v. 8, p. 199.

Isa. 59:2, margin. Sin separates from God.

Rom. 3:20; 7:7. The law points out sin.

Jas. 1:23-25. A spiritual mirror; reveals sin, but can not remove it. T., v. 4, p. 294.

1 John 1:7, 9. Blood of Christ alone can cleanse from sin.

Gal. 3:24. Law leads to Christ. D. A. 308.

Rom. 3:31. Faith establishes the law. D. A. 126.

Isa. 51:7; Ps. 37:31. Law in the heart establishes righteousness.

Rom. 3:21. Law witnesses to righteousness.

Eccl. 12:13, 14; Rom. 2:12, 13. Standard in judgment. G. C. 482.

Rev. 22:14. Passport into glory. G. C. 639, 640.

Ps. 119:97. "O how I love thy law."

CITY WORK

"Behold the cities, and their need of the gospel! . . . Who are carrying a burden for the large cities? A few have felt the burden, but in comparison with the great need and the many oppor-

Gen. 19:17.

Gen. 19:17-20. Ruin of daughters, Gen. 19.
Deceit and violence, Ps. 55:9-11. If Satan is not
destroyed, he will fill the face of the earth with
cities, Isa. 14:20, 21. Cities judged, Eze. 22:2. According to light, Matt. 11:20-24. In the day of God,
Zeph. 1:14-16; Isa. 30:25. Complete destruction,
Isa. 32:19; Jer. 4:26; Rev. 16:17-19.

City Work under God's Direction

One entire book is devoted to missionary work
in a great city.

Jonah 1:1-3. One lone worker; refused to go. P. K.
266.

Jonah 1:4-17. God prepared a fish to save Jonah.
P. K. 267, 268.

Jonah 2:1-9. In his strange prison Jonah learned
five fundamental principles underlying *all
successful* missionary efforts in great cities.
P. K. 269.

1. Prayer must ascend *into* God's temple.
Jonah 2:7.

2. "They that observe *lying vanities* forsake
their own mercy."

3. Sacrifice with the *voice of thanksgiving.*
Jonah 2:9.

4. Pay *all* vows. Jonah 2:9.

5. "Salvation *is of the Lord.*" Jonah 2:9.

4

Jonah 2:10. When Jonah learned these lessons he was ready for city work.

Jonah 3:1-4. He then went with God's message instead of his own.

Jonah 3:5-10. Great success followed. P. K. 270, 271.

The five principles have lost none of their power. P. K. 274, 275.

Christ and the Apostles as City Missionaries

Matt. 9:35. Jesus worked all the cities.

Matt. 4:23, 24. Health work opened doors.

Luke 10:1. Workers went two and two into every city.

Luke 10:9. Cared for the sick.

Acts 8:5-7. First city worker after the crucifixion. A. A. 106, 107.

Acts 13:42-45. Open air meetings, since no synagogue could hold almost the whole city. A. A. 171-174.

Acts 19:1-7. Work in Ephesus a sample.

Acts 18:18-24. Bible workers prepared the way.

Acts 19:8. Three months' public effort unsuccessful. A. A. 285.

Acts 19:9, 10. Did not leave, but changed methods; taught in school for two years. A. A. 286.

Acts 19:10. Great success followed.

Acts 19:18, 19. Genuine reformation. A. A. 287, 288.

Acts 19:23-28. Idolatry tottered throughout almost all Asia.

Acts 19:29-35. Idolaters created riot.

Acts 19:36, 37. In quieting riot, town clerk said

city. G. W. 299, old edition; T., v. 9, pp. 109, 124.

NATURE OF MAN

"To the Christian, death is but a sleep, a moment of silence and darkness." D. A. 787.

What Is Death?

Ps. 13:3. The psalmist calls death a sleep.

1 Thess. 4:15. The dead are asleep. D. A. 787.

Matt. 27:52. They sleep in their graves.

Acts 13:36. When David died he went to sleep.

1 Cor. 15:51. Paul calls death a sleep.

1 Thess. 4:14. The righteous dead sleep in Jesus.

1 Kings 11:43. More than twenty-five times the expression, "Slept with his fathers," is used when recording deaths of kings in the old Testament. We give one sample text.

John 11:11-14. *Jesus calls death a sleep.*

Heb. 9:27. One death is appointed unto men.

Gen. 2:17; 3:22-24; Rom. 6:23. Death is the result of sin.

John 8:44. Satan is the father of sin.

Heb. 2:14. He has the power of death.

2 Tim. 1:10. Christ abolished death. He changed death into a sleep.

1 Cor. 15:22. This included *all* the dead.

John 5:25-28. Christ has the power to awaken all from the sleep of death. D. A. 320.

Are the Dead Conscious?

Ps. 146:4. "His breath goeth forth; . . . in that very day his thoughts perish."

Job 14:12, 21. No knowledge of what happens on earth after death. G. C. 549.

Isa. 38:10, 11. Do not see the Lord or men on the earth. G. C. 546.

Eccl. 9:5, 6. Do not know anything. D. A. 557, 558.

Ps. 115:17. Praise not the Lord.

Ps. 6:5. No remembrance of God.

Ps. 88:11, 12. Grave the land of forgetfulness.

Job 14:12. Remain in the grave till the heavens are no more.

Rev. 6:14-17. Heavens roll together when Christ returns to earth.

Job 19:23-27. Job knew he would awake at that time.

John 5:29. Two classes in the resurrection.

1 Thess. 4:16, 17. Righteous arise when Christ comes.

Rev. 20:5. Wicked raised 1000 years later.

How Are the Dead Raised Up?

1 Cor. 15:35. "With what body do they come?"

1 Cor. 15:36-38. The same individual will come from the grave that went into the grave, as truly as wheat comes from wheat sown in the earth.

1 Cor. 15:44. "It is sown a natural body; it is raised a spiritual body."

John 20:15, 16. Mary knew her Lord by His voice.

John 20:3-8. John recognized Christ by His orderly habits.

John 20:26-28. Philip knew Him by His personal appearance. As Jesus' friends recognized Him, so we will recognize our friends.

1 Cor. 15:51-54. Righteous dead raised immortal.

Phil. 3:20, 21. Their bodies will be like Christ's glorious body.

Matt. 17:1, 2. Their faces will shine as the sun, and raiment be white as the light.

Hos. 13:14. Christ has pledged to redeem them from death.

Job 14:15. He will call, the saints will answer.

Isa. 26:19. Christ will call, "Awake and sing."

1 Cor. 15:54-57. The righteous spring forth with a song of victory. T., v. 2, p. 229.

Two Resurrections and the Second Death

John 5:28, 29. Two resurrections,—one to life and the other to damnation. G. C. 544.

Rev. 20:5. One thousand years between the two.

Matt. 24:30, 31. When the righteous arise Christ gathers them.

Rev. 20:5-9. When the wicked arise Satan gathers them. C. O. L. 270.

Rev. 20:13. Gathered from land and sea.

Rev. 20:6; 2:11. Righteous never die the second death.

Rev. 20:14. Second death is the lake of fire.

Rev. 20:15; Rom. 6:23. All whose names are not in the book of life, suffer the second death.

Eternal Life, the Gift of God

1 Tim. 6:15, 16. God only hath immortality.

John 5:26. God gave Christ immortality.

1 John 5:11, 12. Eternal life given man through Christ. "He that hath the Son hath life; and he that hath not the Son hath not life."

1 John 3:15. No wicked person hath eternal life.

2 Tim. 1:10. Christ "brought life and immortality to light."

Job 4:17. Man is only mortal.

Rom. 2:6, 7. We are admonished to *seek for immortality, eternal life.* If we possessed it, we would not need to seek for it.

1 Cor. 15:51-54. It will be given the righteous at Christ's second coming.

Life Only through Christ, as Taught by the Cities of Refuge

Num. 35:11-14. The six cities of refuge were a constant reminder that eternal life was a gift and not an inherent human inheritance. P. P. 516.

Deut. 19:2, 3. The roads leading to the cities were to be kept in good repair that the one fleeing might not be hindered. P. P. 515.

Heb. 6:4-6; Matt. 12:31, 32. There is an unpardonable sin.

Heb. 12:16, 17. Illustrated in the case of Esau.

Joshua 20:4. Confession was made at the gate before the one fleeing was received.

1 John 1:9. The sinner must confess.

Num. 35:26-29. Inside the city was life; outside the city was death. P. P. 517.

Prov. 18:10; Ps. 91:2. Christ is a refuge. P. P. 516, 517.

1 John 5:11, 12; John 15:4-7. Our safety is to abide in Christ.

Num. 35:26-28. If one presumptuously went outside the city, his life could be taken.

Eze. 18:24-26. The one that turns from the refuge of Christ, dies the second death.

Joshua 20:6; Num. 35:25. There were two important events to which the dweller in the city looked forward,—the judgment and the death of the high priest. The judgment decided his destiny; the death of the high priest restored him to freedom of the land. The decision in the judgment decides our eternal destiny; and when our High Priest ceases to be high priest, our adversary, the devil, has no power to take our life, and we come into possession of our eternal inheritance.

THE GREAT ADVERSARY

"The true character of the usurper, and his real object, must be understood by all."

First Fall of Satan

Eze. 28:15. Was perfect when created.

Eze. 28:12. Full of wisdom, perfect in beauty. P. P. 35.

Eze. 28:14. Covering cherub.

Eze. 28:17. Proud of his beauty.

Eze. 28:17. Pride ruined his wisdom.

Isa. 14:13. Coveted higher position. P. P. 36.

Isa. 14:14. Coveted the throne of God.

Rev. 12:7. Other angels affected. P. P. 37, 39; T., v. 3, p. 328.

Rev. 12:7. Christ and loyal angels fought against Satan and his angels.

Rev. 12:8. Satan was defeated.

Isa. 14:12. Satan cast out of heaven. D. A. 493.

Rev. 12:9. His angels cast out with him. P. P. 41.

Rev. 12:9. Cast to this earth.

Gen. 3:1-6. He caused our first parents to sin. P. P. 53-59.

Rom. 6:16. Gained Adam's dominion.

Eph. 2:2. Prince of the power of the air.

John 14:30. The Saviour called him the prince of this world. D. A. 123, 679.

Job 1:7. He represented the earth in the council.

Job 1:9-11. Accused God of being arbitrary.

Job 1:12-22. When given power only destroyed.

John 14:30. Satan has no part in Christ, who was
a sinless son of Adam.

John 12:31-33. Christ's death judged Satan. D. A.
490.

John 12:31. Christ's death cast Satan out of his
place.

Luke 10:18. He fell as lightning from heaven.

Rev. 12:10. A shout rang through heaven when
the accuser was cast out.

2 Peter 2:19; Heb. 2:14. Christ overcame Satan,
and is now the representative of this world.

Heb. 2:17. Instead of the accuser at the gate of
heaven, we have a merciful High Priest.

Heb. 4:14-16. One who loves to be merciful to
us.

Third Fall of Satan

Rev. 20:1-3. It does not take Christ or a host of
angels to overcome Satan; one angel binds him.

Rev. 20:3. He is confined to his own territory.

Jer. 4:23-26; Isa. 24:19-21. Sin has made the earth
a dark abyss.

1 Thess. 4:16, 17. Righteous in heaven.

Jer. 25:31-33. Wicked all dead.

Rev. 20:3. Satan is alone with the evil angels for 1000 years. He is bound by circumstances; the righteous are in heaven, the wicked dead, there is no one for him to tempt.

Rev. 20:5. The wicked live again at the end of 1000 years.

Rev. 20:7. This gives Satan work, and he is said to be "loosed."

Rev. 20:8. Deceives the wicked.

Rev. 20:9. As they gather for battle all are destroyed.

Heb. 2:14. Christ died to destroy Satan.

Rev. 20:10. As long as Satan lives in the fire he suffers torment, but as sure as Christ died, Satan will die when he has suffered the penalty for sin.

Eze. 28:18, 19. Satan becomes ashes on the earth in the sight of the righteous. D. A. 490.

Mal. 4:1-3. Ashes on the new earth is all that remains of Satan and sinners.

Ancient Spiritualism

Ex. 7:11-13. Sorcerers (spiritualist mediums) influenced Pharaoh.

Lev. 19:31; 20:6, 27; Ex. 22:18; Deut. 18:10-12. Spiritualist mediums, anciently called witches and wizards, were an abomination. G. C. 556.

2 Kings 1:1-4. Consulted in case of sickness. T., v. 5, pp. 191-199.

1 Sam. 28:8, 11. Familiar spirits profess to be spirits of dead people.

tions wo...

iar spirits.

2 Kings 17:16, 17. Spiritualism always connected with Baal- or sun-worship.

Deut. 32:17; Ps. 106:37; Lev. 17:7. The heathen Baal-worship was devil-worship. This was the principal adversary against the cause of God until about the sixth century A. D.

Gen. 3:1-6. The first spiritualist medium was the serpent. The devil spoke directly through the serpent.

Isa. 8:19, 20. When asked to consult with familiar spirits, turn to the law and to the testimony.

Modern Spiritualism

Rev. 16:13-15. Unclean spirits will speak through great powers of earth in the last days.

Rev. 13:1-14. As the prophetic period of 1260 years was closing, a nation was seen arising. The United States arose at that time. Out of this nation a miracle-working power was to arise. About 1848 modern spiritualism began to attract attention through the Fox sisters of New York.

Acts 8:9; 13:6-10; Rev. 9:20, 21. Sorcery was an evil in New Testament times.

Rev. 18:2. Modern Babylon becomes "the hold of
every foul spirit."

1 Cor. 10:20. Gentiles worshiped devils.

Job. 14:14, 20, 21; 7:8-10. The dead do not know
what takes place after their death.

Ps. 146:3, 4. Their power to think ceases.

Eccl. 9:5, 6. The dead do not know anything;
hence, a spirit purporting to be a spirit of any
dead person, must be a wicked spirit trying to
deceive.

Rev. 16:14; 13:14. The devil can work miracles.
G. C. 553, 554.

2 Cor. 11:13-15. The devil can appear as an angel
of light; hence, can easily personate the dead.
G. C. 552.

Rev. 16:13-15. Spiritualism will be a bond uniting
different earthly powers together for the "battle of that great day of God Almighty." T.,
v. 5, p. 451.

HOLY SPIRIT

"The Spirit of God, received into the soul, will
quicken all its faculties. Under the guidance of
the Holy Spirit, the mind that is devoted unre-
servedly to God, develops harmoniously, and is
strengthened to comprehend and fulfill the requirements of God. The weak, vacillating character
becomes changed to one of strength and steadfast-
ness." D. A. 251.

Efficiency of the Holy Spirit

Gen. 1:2. Divine agency in creation.

John 14:16, 17. Connecting link between God and
man. A. A. 50.

John 10:8-11. ...
eousness. A. A. 120, 49.

Rom. 8:26, 27. Presents our prayers.

Rom. 8:27, 28. Makes all work for good to the
faithful.

John 14:26. Comforter; strengthens memory. D. A.
670.

Eze. 36:26, 27; 1 Sam. 10:6, 9. Changes the
heart.

Acts 1:8. Gives power. D. A. 672.

Acts 2:4. Gives utterance.

Eph. 4:30. We are sealed by the Spirit.

Receiving the Holy Spirit

Luke 11:8. Desire the Spirit. T., v. 6, p. 90.

Luke 11:9-13. Promise of the Spirit ten times repeated.

Zech. 10:1. Pray for it. A. A. 55, 56.

2 Sam. 23:2-4. A precious experience. E. 95.

Gal. 5:22-25. Receiver bears 9 kinds of fruit. T.,
v. 5, p. 169.

Isa. 11:2, 3. Seven manifestations,—wisdom, etc.

Ex. 28:2-5; 35:30-35. It will help in every lawful
line of business.

John 20:22, 23. Receiver is God's representative.

Luke 24:44, 45. Opens minds to comprehend the Scriptures.

Heb. 6:4-6. Fatal to reject. D. A. 587.

Isa. 55:1. Received without money.

Joel 2:23-25. Restores wasted life. E. 106.

John 6:63. Words are Spirit.

John 1:1, 2, 14. God, Christ, and the Word, synonymous.

Heb. 4:12-16. One does not work independently of the other.

Acts 10:44-48. When Peter was explaining the Scriptures, the Holy Ghost was poured out.

Acts 1:15-26. The study of the 109th Psalm, and regulating their lives by it, brought the Spirit on Pentecost. D. A. 827.

Heb. 4:12, 13. The word of God with the Holy Spirit searches the deepest recesses of the heart.

How to Retain the Spirit

Acts 8:17-23. Can not be purchased.

1 Cor. 3:16, 17. Will not dwell in a defiled body.

Dan. 1:8. Improper food defiles body.

Luke 1:15. Will not abide with strong drink.

Jude 19. Will not dwell with sensuality.

Gal. 5:16, 17. Contrary to lust of flesh.

1 Cor. 2:14. Does not dwell in the natural heart.

Eze. 36:26, 27. God gives the Spirit. A. A. 47, 48.

Rom. 8:15. Pledge of adoption.

Eph. 4:30, 31. Do not grieve it. D. A. 490.

Acts 5:3, 4, 9. Do not try to deceive it.

15. Why wi............
Deut. 32:2. A blessing, Ps. 72:6, 7. ....
blessing, Eze. 34:26. Showers of righteousness, Isa.
45:8. Floods, Isa. 44:3. Result, Isa. 44:4, 5. When
sent, Isa. 44:3; Ps. 68:9. When a special out-
pouring, Acts 2:17, 18. How compared with former
rain, Joel 2:23. Why latter rain is withheld, Jer.
5:23-27. Sins that withhold the blessing, Jer. 3:
1-3; Mal. 3:8-11; Eze. 22:24-26. Judgments sent,
Amos 4:6-11. Prepare to meet God, Amos 4:12.
Response, Hos. 6:1-3. Repent, Acts 3:19-21. How
literal rain is received, Job 29:23. Same desire for
spiritual, Ps. 42:1, 2; 119:131. Promise, Ps. 81:10.
After conditions are met, pray, Zech. 10:1. Pray till
we receive, Hos. 10:12. Model prayer, Jer. 14:20-
22. Elijah's experience repeated, Mal. 4:5, 6. Why
rain withheld, 1 Kings 18:18. Elijah's work, 1
Kings 18:21. Test, 1 Kings 18:24; Matt. 3:11. Result of prayer, 1 Kings 18:38, 39. Preparatory work,
1 Kings 18:40. This preparation sign of rain, 1
Kings 18:41. Then he prayed, 1 Kings 18:42-44.
Result, 1 Kings 18:45, 46. Reward for waiting, Isa.
40:31. What will the remnant be, Micah 5:7. Effect
of the latter rain upon the life, Joel 2:23-27. The
Lord waiting, Jas. 5:7; E. W. 71, 86, 271, 279;
G. C. 611-613.

The Loud Cry

Num. 14:12-21. When Moses plead for Israel, God answered his prayer and promised that "all the earth shall be filled with the glory of God." This is the first promise of the loud cry.

Ps. 72:19. David repeats the promise.

Isa. 6:3. An heavenly seraphim assures Isaiah of the promise.

Isa. 11:9. Isaiah repeats it.

Hab. 2:14. Again the promise is given.

Eze. 43:2. Ezekiel saw the earth shining with the glory of God.

Rev. 18:1, 2. John also saw the earth lightened with the glory of God. He heard the mighty cry of the angel in charge of this work. Six prophets of God have been permitted to see this great work which will be accomplished before Christ returns to the earth. T., v. 9, pp. 154, 209; v. 8, pp. 19-21; E. W. 37, 27, 277.

PROPHECY

"In the annals of human history the growth of nations, the rise and fall of empires, appear as dependent upon the will and prowess of man. The shaping of events seems, to a great degree, to be determined by his power, ambition, or caprice. But in the word of God the curtain is drawn aside, and we behold, behind, above, and through all the play and counter-play of human interests and power and passions, the agencies of the all-merciful One, silently, patiently working out the counsels of His own will. The Bible reveals the true philosophy of history." E. 173.

Job 12:…
Hab. 1:5-11; P. K. 499, 500.

Dan. 4:13-17. God watches over the nations. P. K. 536, 537.

Eze. 29:17-20. God uses one nation to punish other nations.

Jer. 25:9-11. God calls even heathen nations His servants to do His bidding. Jer. 50:11-20.

Dan. 10:20. When the angels of the Lord left the court of Media and Persia, Grecia arose.

Jer. 46:17. When God forsakes a kingdom, it is but a "noise"; it soon passes.

Jer. 29:5-7. Seek the peace of the country where you live.

Matt. 22:17-21. It is lawful to pay tribute. D. A. 601, 602.

Matt. 17:24-27. Jesus performed a miracle to pay an unjust tax rather than offend. D. A. 432-435.

Gen. 39:7-9; 50:24, 25; 41:39-46. Joseph was true to God while filling a high position under the Egyptian government. P. P. 210-223.

Dan. 6:1-5. Daniel was prime minister of Media and Persia. P. K. 487, 488.

Dan. 6:16-23. He was always true to God while loyal to his government.

Dan. 6:28; 2:48. Daniel was a government official for over 70 years.

Esther 4:1-17; 10:3. Mordecai was true to God and at the same time was judge (sat in the gate) under the Medo-Persian empire. P. K. 600-606.

Titus 3:1. Be subject to the principalities and powers; also be ready for every good work.

1 Peter 2:13-15. The Christian's willing obedience to the government will "put to silence the ignorance of foolish men."

1 Peter 2:16, 17. The servants of God will honor the ruler of the nation.

Dan. 3:1-26. The three Hebrews would not disobey God, but they were faithful servants of the nation in every way where its laws did not conflict with God's laws. Dan. 2:49; 3:12, 30; P. K. 508-513, 548.

1 Tim. 2:1-3. Paul said it "was good and acceptable in the sight of God" to pray for rulers. Nero, who was a synonym for cruelty, was then ruling. If that was pleasing to God, how much more should we pray for the rulers of our own country who fear God.

Second Chapter of Daniel

Dan. 2:1-9. The story of the dream.

Dan. 2:10-13. The failure of the wise men to interpret the dream. P. K. 491-493.

Dan. 2:14-16. Daniel's interview with the king. P. K. 493, 501.

Dan. 2:17, 18. Prayer for the interpretation. P. K. 493, 494.

Isa. ... ...

years before his birth. P. K. ...

Isa. 44:27; Jer. 50:38; 51:36. Bed of the river dry. P. K. 552, 553, 531.

Jer. 51:46. In 539 B. C., the rumor; in 538 B. C., the overthrow.

Dan. 5:30, 31. Kingdom given Darius. Give a brief description of the taking of Babylon by Cyrus. P. K., chapter 43.

Isa. 13:19-22. Site of Babylon at the present day. P. K. 531-533.

Dan. 2:39. Third universal kingdom.

Dan. 8:20, 21. Grecia followed Medo-Persia.

Dan. 2:40. Fourth universal kingdom.

Luke 2:1; John 11:48. Rome a universal kingdom. The names of three kingdoms were given in the Old Testament; hence, Rome must be the fourth.

Dan. 2:41, 42. Clay mingled with iron denotes division. Between the years 356 and 483, Rome was divided into ten parts. Some kingdoms strong, others weak.

Dan. 2:43. Never another universal kingdom.

Dan. 2:44. They remain in a divided state until the kingdom of God is set up.

Dan. 2:45. The dream is certain.

2 Peter 1:5-11. A godly life will gain an abundant
entrance into the everlasting kingdom of our
Lord and Saviour, Jesus Christ.

The Gospel Preached in the Great Universal Kingdoms of the Earth

Each kingdom had a knowledge of the true God,
proclaimed not only by faithful living but by individuals who loved the truth more than life.

Dan. 1:1-20; 2:48, 49. Faithful living in Babylon.

Dan. 3:16-26. Love God more than life. P. K. 508,
509.

Dan. 3:2, 3, 27-29. World-wide proclamation of the
truth. P. K. 510, 511.

Dan. 5:1-4. Light rejected.

Dan. 5:5-9, 24-28. God vindicated. P. K. 524-
533.

Dan. 10:20. Angel left Babylon.

Dan. 6:1-5. Faithful living in Medo-Persia. P. K.
539, 542.

Dan. 6:16-23. Loved God more than life. P. K. 543,
544, 556, 557.

Dan. 6:25-27. World-wide proclamation of the
truth.

Esther 3:7-15. God rejected in Medo-Persia. P. K.
502.

Esther 4:1-17. Esther loved God more than life.

Esther 8:15-17. World-wide proclamation of the
truth.

We have little Bible history of the period of
Grecian supremacy. Josephus tells us that Alex-
ander the Great was shown the prophecies of Daniel relating to himself. Dan. 8:20; 10:20.

world.

Eccl. 1:9. As in the past, the work will be done by those who love God more than life.

Characteristics of the Five Great Universal Kingdoms

Dan. 2:35. Every kingdom represented in the end of time.

Hab. 1:6, 11; Dan. 4:28-31. Leading sins of Babylon, —pride and exalting man rather than God. P. K. 501, 502.

Rev. 17:1-4; 18:7-20. Same spirit in modern Babylon. G. C. 388, 384, 385.

Isa. 13:16-18. Medo-Persia cruel.

Esther 3:8-15. Decree to destroy all of God's people. P. K. 600.

Esther 4:1-16. God saved His people. P. K. 601-604.

Rev. 13:15-17. Similar decree will be made. P. K. 605, 606; G. C. 635.

Rev. 15:1, 2. God will deliver His people. G. C. 636.

1 Cor. 1:22; 2 Cor. 10:5, margin; Acts 17:16-22; 2 Tim. 3:7. Exalting reason above God's word, sin of ancient Greece. Same spirit is mani-

fested in higher criticism at the present day. E. 227.

Dan. 7:25. All four nations persecuted the people of God more or less, but *Rome only* presumed to *change the law of God.*

Rev. 13:14; Isa. 30:8-12, margin. Same spirit manifest in the closing history of the world. P. K. 187, 188.

Dan. 2:35. Gold,—pride, self-exaltation; silver,—cruelty, and over-bearing spirit; brass,—exalt man's reason above the word of God; iron,—change God's law to suit the mind of man. Any of these characteristics cherished in the heart means utter destruction, when God destroys all nations.

Isa. 42:8. God demands full surrender. P. K. 189.

Seventh Chapter of Daniel

In this line of prophecy the character of the kingdoms is represented under the symbols of different beasts.

Dan. 7:2. Striving winds and a turbulent sea.

Dan. 11:40; Zech. 7:14. Winds denote war.

Rev. 17:15. Water denotes multitudes and nations.

Dan. 7:3. Beasts diverse one from another.

Dan. 7:4. Babylon represented by a lion.

Jer. 50:17. Same symbol used forty years before.

Hab. 1:6-8. Wings denote rapid conquest.

Jer. 17:9. Man's heart denotes wickedness,—nation ready for destruction.

Isa. 13:17, 18. More than 100 years before, Isaiah said Medes were cruel.

Dan. 7:5. When Daniel saw the bear arise, devour-

Dan. 7:17, 18. Four kingdoms followed by God's kingdom.

Dan. 9:2, 3. Daniel was a student of the prophecies and understood the first three symbols.

Dan. 7:19-23. He asks about the fourth.

Dan. 7:23. Fourth beast, fourth kingdom.

Luke 2:1. Rome, the fourth kingdom.

Dan. 7:24. Ten divisions; divided between 356 and 483 A. D.

Dan. 7:24. A different power arises after the division and subdues three kings. The papacy arose in 538; Heruli, Ostrogoths, and Vandals overthrown to make way for it.

Dan. 7:25. Character of the power and length of supremacy. G. C. 439.

Dan. 11:13, margin; Rev. 13:5; 12:6; Num. 14:34. Explain the period of 1260 years. G. C. 54, 55.

Seven Trumpets

Christ lived and died, and the Christian religion was proclaimed to the world all within the confines of the Roman Empire; therefore it is only reasonable to expect that the downfall of Rome, which was so closely connected with the history of Christ's church, should be a subject of prophecy.

The first four trumpets deal with the breaking up of western Rome; the last three, with the overthrow of eastern Rome.

Num. 10:9. Trumpet ancient summons to war.

Rev. 8:2. Seven angels given charge of this prophecy.

Rev. 8:6, 7. Hordes of barbarians of N. Asia on account of trouble with China turned westward and poured into the Roman territory.

The Goths, under Alaric and two other organized bodies of barbarians, led the raids. A. D. 410, Alaric sacked Rome. About 407 A. D., seven barbarian nations had taken their places as follows: *Franks*, northern France; *Vandals*, Spain, later N. Africa; *Visigoths*, S. France and Spain; *Burgundians*, Switzerland and part of France and Germany; *Suevi*, Portugal and N. W. Spain; *Ostrogoths*, Italy; *Huns*, S. W. Russia. Gibbon's Rome, chapters 30, 31.

Rev. 8:8. From 429 to 468 A. D., Genseric, leading the Vandals of N. Africa, made repeated attacks on the Roman Empire, destroying large fleets of vessels. So terrible was this warfare, that "Vandalism" is still a synonym for ruthless destruction. Gibbon's Rome, chapters 33, 37.

Rev. 8:10, 11. The Huns, led by Attila, made fierce attacks in the regions of the Alps; Chalons was greatest battle. Attila's raids from 451 to 453 A. D., were finished 15 years before Genseric ceased to harass Rome from the South.

After Attila's war, the Heruli settled in Italy, the Lombards in the N. of Italy, and the last of the ten divisions, the Anglo-Saxons, in England, about 471 A. D. Gibbon's Rome, chapter 35.

13th century, Othman founded a government; and July 27, 1299, he entered Nicomedia,—the first attack of the Ottoman government on eastern Rome. Gibbon's Rome. They were to hurt men five months,—150 years. July 27, 1299, plus 150 years, equals July 27, 1449.

Rev. 9:12-21. The four sultanies of Aleppo, Iconium, Damascus, and Bagdad, were the central strength of the Ottoman Empire. In 1449, John Palæologus, the Greek emperor, died; his brother, Deacozes, would not take the throne without the consent of Amurath, the Turkish sultan. Thus the power of the Turkish Empire was loosed. It was loosed for a day, a month, and a year, or for 391 years, 15 days; they were to have full power. July 27, 1449, plus 391 years, 15 days, equals Aug. 11, 1840. G. C. 334.

Rev. 9:13-21. To save Turkey from being overthrown by Egypt, Turkey accepted the intervention of England, Russia, Austria, and Prussia. An ultimatum was drawn up by the great powers which pledged themselves to coerce Egypt, if Egypt refused to accept the

terms. As long as the sultan held the ultimatum, he still maintained his independence;
but as soon as the document was in the hands
of Mehemet Ali, it was beyond the sultan's
power to control the situation. The document
was put into the power of Mehemet Ali, and
disposed of according to his orders, Aug. 11,
1840. Since then Turkey has been "the sick
man of the East." G. C. 334, 335.

Rev. 11:14. The 3rd woe did not *immediately* follow the 2nd, but came *quickly*.

Rev. 10:7; 11:15. The finishing of the work, or
the third angel's message, which would be
finished under the 7th trumpet, began in 1844
A. D.

Note.—For a full explanation of the woe trum-
pets, see "Prophetic Exposition," published 1842, by
Josiah Litch; also "An Exposition of the Seven
Trumpets," *Review and Herald, 1875.*

SEVEN CHURCHES

There were many Christian churches in Asia
during the first century of the Christian era; and
God chose seven of them to represent the seven
periods of His church during the remainder of time.

Ephesus

Time,—first century; meaning,—first, or desirable.

The New Testament gives church history covering the 1st century; therefore, the fulfillment of
the prophecy is found in the history given. T.,
v. 6, pp. 422, 423.

Rev. 2:1-7. Work, Acts 20:20; 5:42; 6:2-4; 9:36-40.

Jude 21-23. Listening ear, Isa. 50:4, 5; Isa.
40:6. Overcomer's reward, Rev. 22:1, 2; Isa.
66:22, 23.

Smyrna

Time,—100-323 A. D.; meaning,—myrrh, or sweet
smelling savor.

Rev. 2:8-11. Works, tribulation, and poverty, John
15:20; Jas. 2:5; Acts 20:29-31; 2 Peter 2:1.
Ten days: this doubtless refers to the persecution of ten years under Diocletian, the emperor of Rome, 302-312 A. D. Crown of life,
Rev. 1:18. Overcomer's reward, Rev. 20:6.

Pergamos

Time,—about 323 A. D.-538 A. D.; meaning,—
height, elevation.

Rev. 2:12-17. Leading sin,—holding doctrine of Balaam; brief study of the doctrine and character of Balaam, P. P. 438-452. True to God
in the beginning, Num. 22:18. Loved wages of
unrighteousness, 2 Peter 2:14, 15. God gave him
a free choice, Num. 22:20. His way perverse,
Num. 22:32. Balaam reproved, 2 Peter 2:16.
United Baal-, or sun-worship, with the wor-

ship of the true God, Num. 23:1-3. Hired to work against God's people, Deut. 23:3, 4. United with the king to overthrow the people of God, Rev. 2:14. Honor and position offered him, Num. 22:17. Balaam died a soothsayer, fighting against the people of God. Joshua 13:22.

Balaam's history is parallel history with the church from about 323 to 538 A. D. The church entered this period a pure church, but united with the state, substituted "the venerable day of the sun" for the true Sabbath, and at the end was persecuting the people of God. Heathen customs were introduced into the church under the garb of Christianity. Remember the course of Balaam, Micah 6:5. A woe pronounced upon all who follow the errors of Balaam, Jude 11.

Thyatira

Time,—538 A. D.-1798 A. D.; meaning,—sacrifice of contrition.

Rev. 2:18-29. Teaching of Jezebel, the leading sin, P. K. 114, 115, 215, 204-216. A brief study of the character and sins of Jezebel. Always known as a Baal-worshiper, 1 Kings 16:31. Introduced Baal-worship among the people of God, 1 Kings 16:32. Baal-worship is sun-worship, 2 Kings 23:4, 5, margin; 2 Chron. 14: 5, margin; Jer. 43:13, margin; 44:15-19. Jezebel introduced heathen customs, 1 Kings 21:25, 26. Jezebel's manner of dressing, 2 Kings 9: 30. She destroyed the people of God, 1 Kings 18:4, 13. Given opportunity to repent, 1 Kings 21:27-29; 18:17-46. Repented not, 1 Kings 19:

corrupt church, ...

exalteth itself above God, 2 Thess. 2:1-4. Thinks to change the law of God; the day of the sun, or Sunday, was substituted for the Sabbath of the Lord, Dan. 7:25. The woman (church) guides the beast (civil power), Rev. 17:3. The food given by this church abominable and filthy; heathen customs were mingled with the truth during this period, Rev. 17:4. Modern Jezebel's manner of dressing, Rev. 17:4. Destroyed the people of God, Rev. 17:6; Dan. 7:25; Rev. 13:7. Opportunity given to repent, Rev. 2:21; 12:16; 18:4. Repented not, Rev. 12:17; 13:16, 17; Dan. 7:21. Cast into tribulation, Rev. 2:22; 18:6-24. Her daughters destroyed. Rev. 2:23; 17:5; 19:20, 21; 2 Thess. 2:8. Before the universe of God, it will be shown that God is true and just, Rev. 2:23; 19:1-3; Phil. 2:9-11. The promise of the coming of the Lord prominent, Rev. 2:25. Noted for their works, Rev. 2:19. The overcomer is the one that keeps God's works unto the end, Rev. 2:26. Our own works must be changed for God's works and ways, Heb. 4:10. The righteous will help to execute judgments upon the wicked, Rev. 2: 26, 27; Ps. 2:7-9; 149:5-9. Wicked left as dung upon the ground, Jer. 25:32, 33. Christ is the morning-star, Rev. 22:16. Christ is received in exchange for our sins, Gal. 1:3, 4. The message is for all who will hear, Rev. 2: 29.

Sardis

Time,—1798-1833; meaning,—song of joy, or that which remains.

Rev. 3:1-6. Admonished to be watchful and repent lest the Lord should come and find them unprepared. Some of this church would live during the judgment. The overcomer would have his name retained in the book of life.

Philadelphia

Time,—1833-1844; meaning,—brotherly love.

Rev. 3:7-14. In preparing to meet their Lord, the church was drawn together. Christ entered the 2nd apartment of the heavenly sanctuary. No combination of earthly circumstances can prevent our entering by faith, for it is beyond the power of man to shut the door. Hypocrites will be exposed, but the faithful ones will be shielded. The overcomers will be pillars in the temple of God.

Laodicea

Time,—1844—? Meaning,—judging a just people.

The Saviour introduces Himself under three titles, Rev. 3:14. Lukewarm, Rev. 3:15, 16.

Dan. 12:1. Close of probation; time of trouble. G. C. 613.

Dan. 12:2. Partial resurrection. G. C. 637.

Dan. 12:3. Soul-winner's reward.

Dan. 12:4. Increase of knowledge.

Dan. 12:5-7. At the end of 1260 years, 1798, the power of the holy people (the Bible) would be scattered. British Bible Society organized 1804; American, 1816.

Dan. 12:8, 9. This period called "the time of the end." Words of Daniel sealed until that time. D. A. 234, 235.

Dan. 12:10. Wise understand the book of Daniel in time of the end. P. K. 547.

Dan. 12:11, margin. Daily (paganism) taken away (508 A. D.) "to set up the abomination" that maketh desolate; 508 A. D. plus 1290 equals 1798 A. D., beginning of the time of the end when the sealed word would be opened and studied. The word "sacrifice" is supplied by man's wisdom, and is not in the text. E. W. 74.

Dan. 12:12. As there is no beginning point given here, we understand the period begins at the same date given in verse 11; 508 A. D. plus 1335 equals 1843 A. D. Then the glad news of Christ's return was proclaimed.

Dan. 12:13. Daniel stands in his lot; his writings studied in time of the end. G. C. 356.

ARMAGEDDON

Rev. 16:16. "Armageddon" occurs but once in the Bible, and then refers to the final battle which closes all earthly scenes. T., v. 6, p. 406.

Joel 3:2, 12. It is generally thought that the battle will be in the "Valley of Jehoshaphat," or the plain of Esdraelon, where noted battles have been fought.

Judges 5:19, 20; Ps. 83:9, 10. The great battle of Megiddo is an object-lesson of the final battle.

2 Chron. 35:22-24. It was here that king Josiah was slain.

Rev. 16:12. The battle of Armageddon takes place under the sixth plague when the river Euphrates is dried up.

Isa. 8:6-8. When a river is used in a figurative sense, it refers to the people living on the border of that river; thus, Turkey is the country referred to by the drying up of the great river Euphrates.

Rev. 16:13, 14. The spirits of devils are one agency in God's hands to gather the whole world to the battle of God Almighty. T., v. 5, p. 451.

Dan. 11:45. The drying up of this river, or the Turkish nation, is equivalent to Turkey's coming to his end with none to help him.

away with a great noise.

Rev. 20:1, 2. Satan and his angels will be the sole dwellers on the earth for 1000 years.

Rev. 20:9-15. Then will come the final battle of all battles.

Rev. 21:1-4. After which there will be "a new heaven and a new earth, wherein dwelleth righteousness."

BUSINESS PRINCIPLES

"Every business transaction is to be fragrant with the presence of God." "Religion and business are not two separate things; they are one."

Rom. 12:17. Be honest in the sight of all men. D. A. 73; T., v. 7, p. 248.

Heb. 13:18. Be willing in all things to live honestly. T., v. 4, p. 285.

Rom. 12:11. Not slothful in business. T., v. 5, p. 178.

Prov. 22:29. Diligence in business wins respect.

1 Thess. 4:11. *Study* to do your own business.

Lev. 19:36. Have just measures and weights.

Prov. 22:22. Never rob nor oppress poor. T., v. 5, p. 350.

5

Ex. 22:22, 23. Never afflict widows or orphans. T., v. 4, pp. 494, 495.

Ex. 22:21. Neither vex nor oppress a stranger. T., v. 6, p. 274.

Lev. 19:13. Pay hired help at the close of each day.

Lev. 19:11. Never steal nor deal falsely. D. A. 556.

Mal. 3:5. God will punish those who do not regard the above principles. T., v. 4, pp. 309, 310.

Jer. 17:11. Ill-gotten riches do not profit. T., v. 4, p. 540.

Jas. 5:1-6. Such riches are corrupted.

Isa. 2:17-20; Rev. 6:15; Prov. 11:4. Riches profit not in the day of wrath.

Luke 12:20, 21. It is foolish to lay up treasure and not be rich toward God.

Mal. 3:8. Some men rob God. T., v. 3, p. 394.

Mal. 3:9. Those who rob God are cursed. T., v. 3, p 269.

Safe Counsel for Business Men

Prov. 3:9, 10. "Honor the Lord with thy substance, and with the first-fruits of *all* thine increase." T., v. 6, p. 384.

Mal. 3:10. Pay an honest tithe. E. 138, 44.

Prov. 22:26. Never be surety for debts.

Prov. 11:15. "He that is surety . . . shall smart for it."

Prov. 6:1, 2. He is snared who is surety for either friend or stranger. T., v. 1, p. 200.

Prov. 17:18. One void of understanding is surety for a friend.

Eccl. 10:10. Never work with blunt tools.

Prov. 27:23. Be diligent in looking after your flocks and herds.

Prov. 11:25. The liberal soul shall be made fat.

Lev. 25:35-37. Never take usury from a poor brother.

Deut. 23:19, 20. You can receive interest on money lent a stranger.

Titus 3:14, margin. Be sure you profess an honest trade. E. 218.

Hab. 2:15. The liquor-seller is cursed.

Prov. 10:4. He becometh poor that deals with a slack hand.

Prov. 20:4. The sluggard shall have nothing.

Prov. 19:15. An idle soul shall suffer hunger.

Prov. 22:16; 28:8. "He that oppresseth the poor to increase his riches . . . shall surely come to want."

Matt. 7:12. Keep the Golden Rule. T., v. 5, p. 335.

Micah 6:8. Do justly, love mercy, and walk humbly with thy God.

Where the Danger Lies

1 Tim. 6:10. *The love of money* is the root of all evil.

Eccl. 5:10. *He that loveth silver* shall not prosper.

Prov. 28:22. He that *hasteth to be rich* hath an evil eye. T., v. 4, p. 351.

Prov. 15:27. He that is *greedy of gain* troubleth his own house. T., v. 4, p. 37.

1 Tim. 6:9. They that *will be rich* fall into temptations, snares, and hurtful lusts.

Ps. 62:10. If riches increase, *set not your heart upon them.* T., v. 3, p. 403.

Jer. 9:23. *Let not the rich man glory in his riches.*

Prov. 11:28. *He that trusteth in his riches shall fall.*

Mark 10:24. *It is hard for them that trust in riches* to enter heaven.

Deut. 8:18. *Never forget that it is God that giveth power to get wealth.* T., v. 2, pp. 278, 279.

Hosea 2:8. Those that *trust in riches,* forget that God increases wealth.

Prov. 23:5. Riches may fly away.

Haggai 1:6-9. God can scatter them if they are not used for His glory. T., v. 2, pp. 281, 282.

1 Sam. 2:7. The Lord maketh poor, and maketh rich.

Prov. 22:2. The rich and the poor meet together, and the Lord is the Maker of them all.

God Honors Both Rich and Poor

Prov. 30:8. "Give me neither poverty nor riches."

Ps. 112:1-5. Wealth and riches will be with those that use them to God's glory.

1 Chron. 4:9, 10. God answers ... ,
    right for temporal prosperity.

Prov. 3:9, 10. The one that honors the Lord with
    his substance can be trusted with wealth.

Ps. 109:30, 31. God stands at the right hand of the
    poor.

Ps. 140:12. God maintains the right of the poor.

Prov. 17:5. He that mocketh the poor reproacheth
    his Maker.

Prov. 28:6. Better to be poor than perverse.

Num. 18:20. Those who attend to the Lord's work
    have no inheritance among the people.

Num. 18:21. They are to be supported from the
    tithe.

Neh. 13:10, 11. When God's workers give their
    attention to worldly business, the work of God
    suffers.

SPIRIT OF PROPHECY

"As the end draws near and the work of giving
the last warning to the world extends, it becomes
more and more important for those who accept
present truth to have a clear understanding of the
nature and influence of the Testimonies, which God

in His providence has linked with the work of the third angel's message from its very rise."—T., v. 5, p. 654.

Visions and Dreams

Job 33:14-18. Dreams given to save from danger.

Gen. 20:3-16. Dream of a Gentile king.

Gen. 37:5-11. Joseph given two dreams.

Gen. 40:5-19. Dreams of Pharaoh's butler and baker.

Gen. 41:1-36. Pharaoh given two dreams.

Joshua 5:13-15; 7:10-15. God appeared several times to Joshua.

Judges 7:13-15. Enemy's dream helped Gideon.

Dan. 2:1-35; 4:13-18. Nebuchadnezzar had two dreams.

Matt. 2:11, 12. Wise men warned by a dream.

Matt. 2:13-15. Joseph obeyed a dream and fulfilled prophecy. Hosea 11:1.

Matt. 2:19, 20. God instructed Joseph in a dream.

Matt. 27:19. Dream of Pilate's wife.

Acts 10:1-7. Cornelius had a vision, but is not called a prophet.

While all true prophets have visions and dreams, that of itself *alone* does not make them prophets.

Prophets and Prophetesses

Num. 11:11-17, 25-29. Seventy prophets associated with Moses, but none did his work.

Num. 12:1-12; Ex. 15:20. Miriam, a prophetess, was not allowed to criticize Moses.

1 Kings 18:13. There were one hundred prophets in Elijah's day; none but Elijah dared meet Ahab. P. K. 147.

Acts 13:1-4. There were prophets at ...
   their work was local.
1 Cor. 14:29-33. Corinthian prophets failed to recognize order among prophets.
1 Cor. 14:36, 37. They were to recognize Paul as a
   leading prophet.

While God may reveal Himself to many, there is
only one leading prophet at any one period of time
upon whom God places the burden of directing His
church.

Leading Prophets

Isa. 63:12. The Lord led Israel by the hand of
   Moses.
Deut. 18:15, 18. Moses was a type of Christ.
Deut. 34:10; Num. 12:7, 8. There was no other
   prophet like Moses.
Ex. 32:32, 33; Hosea 12:13. Moses offered his
   life for the people.
Joshua 1:1-9. Before Moses died on the borders
   of the promised land, he wrote the instruction
   which, if followed, would have led Israel safely
   into the land.
Jer. 15:1. Moses and Samuel had special power
   in prayer for the people.

1 Sam. 7:8, 9; Ps. 99:6. Samuel's prayers saved the people from their enemies.

1 Sam. 3:20; 4:1; 7:5, 6. Samuel was a leading prophet; he led the people.

1 Sam. 3:19. He delivered all of God's words.

Ps. 89:20-37. David's throne, a type of God's throne.

2 Sam. 6:14-19. David was a priest-king. He wore the ephod and offered sacrifices.

1 Kings 17:1. Elijah, the Tishbite, a grand character.

1 Kings 18:4, 17-19. There were one hundred prophets, but only Elijah reproved Ahab.

1 Kings 19:15, 16; 2 Kings 8:12, 13; 9:1-3. Elisha carried forward the work of Elijah; they together completed one great work. P. K. 235.

1 Kings 17:17-23; 2 Kings 4:32-36. Each of these prophets raised the dead; they were both leading prophets.

Mal. 4:4-6; Luke 1:17. Elijah's work was a type of the closing message. Matt. 17:10-13; P. K. 227.

Isaiah was a leading prophet. He also gave testimonies to the surrounding nations. Chapters 13-23.

Jer. 1:1-10. Jeremiah was chosen before his birth. He also was a prophet for the nations.

Jer. 1:17-19. Jeremiah lived in a crisis.

Jer. 7:16; 11:14; 14:11, 17-22. Like Moses and Samuel, he carried a burden for the people, and prayed for them even when God told him not to pray for them.

Luke 7:24-30. John the Baptist, the forerunner of

Spirit of Prophecy in the Remnant Church

Rev. 12:17; 19:10. The remnant keep the law of God and have the Spirit of prophecy.

1 Cor. 12:28. Prophets in Christian church.

Eph. 4:11, 12. Christ left the gift of prophecy in the church.

Ex. 7:1; 4:15, 16. A prophet of the Lord is a spokesman for God.

1 Peter 1:10, 11; 2 Peter 1:20, 21. The Spirit from the Father and Christ speaks through the prophets. Heb. 1:1, 2; T., v. 5, p. 661.

Rev. 1:1. Steps by which revelation comes: 1st, God; 2nd, Christ; 3rd, angel; 4th, the prophet; 5th, given the people.

2 Chron. 36:12; Eze. 3:17; 2 Sam. 23:2. Prophets speak from the mouth of the Lord. T., v. 5, p. 677.

Rev. 1:2. These messages are called the word of God and testimony of Jesus Christ.

1 Cor. 14:1. The best gift.

Eph. 4:11-14. It brings unity of the faith. Luther and Zwingle were both good men; but there was not unity between them, for there was no leading prophet to give them counsel from

God and each followed his own ideas. T., v.
1, p. 86.

Joshua 1:2-9. The power of the message is not less-
ened by the death of the prophet.

Acts 2:16-18. Prophets in the last days.

1 Cor. 1:4-8. The Spirit of prophecy confirmed in
one gives efficiency, and prepares them for the
coming of the Lord.

Physical Tests of a True Prophet

Num. 12:6. Will have visions.

Dan. 10:8. In vision lose their strength.

Dan. 10:18. Strengthened by the angel.

Dan. 10:17. No breath.

Dan. 10:15. Dumb.

Dan. 10:16. Lips touched by angel.

Dan. 10:16. Speak without breath.

Jer. 1:9. God's words in their mouth. T., v. 5, p.
677.

2 Sam. 23:2. God controls their tongue.

Num. 24:16. Eyes open in vision.

Num. 23:20. Can not reverse the words.

2 Cor. 12:2-4. Unconsciousness of surroundings.

Visions are given in presence of witnesses, who
bear testimony to the fulfillment of the tests.

Characteristics of a True Prophet

Matt. 24:24. There will be false prophets.

1 John 4:1. Test all prophets.

1 John 4:2, 3. Must confess Christ came in the
flesh.

Isa. 8:20. Tested by the law and the testimony.
The words of a true prophet will harmonize
with the law of God and the testimony of all

Num. 12:6.

Dan. 10:7; Acts 9:7, 8. Open or public with witnesses present. T., v. 1, pp. 58, 70.

1 John 1:1-3; 2 Peter 1:16. Witnesses relate what they have seen.

1 Sam. 3:1-10; Dan. 2:19; 7:1. Night visions and dreams. T., v. 1, p. 569.

Acts 9:3. A great light encircles them. T., v. 9, p. 66.

Acts 10:9, 10; Dan. 9:20-23. Vision given while praying. T., v. 5, p. 68.

Eze. 8:3; Dan. 8:2. Taken to other places while in vision. T., v. 5, p. 68; E. W. 32.

Matt. 7:15-20. Known by fruits. T., v. 5, p. 671.

Jer. 7:13, 25; 25:4. Early risers. T., v. 5, p. 67.

Acts 13:8-11; 2 Chron. 20:14-19. God sometimes speaks through a prophet without a vision. T., v. 5, p. 678.

Jer. 23:16. Never flatter.

Acts 11:27-30. Warn of danger.

Acts 15:1, 2, 27-29. Settle doctrinal questions. T., v. 1, pp. 76, 86; E. W. 74, 75.

Acts 16:4, 5. Testimony establishes churches.

Acts 16:6-10. Directs the laborers. E. W. 63.

2 Kings 8:9-12. Countenance of persons reminds

the prophet of what he has seen. T., v. 5, pp. 65, 671.

2 Kings 4:27. Everything is not always revealed.

2 Kings 5:20-26. Reveal unexpressed desires of the heart.

Isa. 38:1-5. Prayers and tears change a testimony. P. K. 340, 341.

Jer. 18:7-10. Principle governing all testimonies.

2 Chron. 21:12, margin. Testimonies written before time for their delivery.

2 Peter 1:20. Every word far-reaching.

Isa. 44:26. God confirms the words. E. W. 59.

Jer. 36:32. Never take back their testimony, but rather add to it. T., v. 5, p. 677.

Doubters' Criticism of Prophets

Num. 12:1-10; Deut. 24:9. Miriam was not pleased with Moses' wife. P. P. 382, 383.

Num. 12:11-16. God punished Miriam.

Num. 22:12, 20. The Lord changed His word.

Eze. 14:4, 5; 2 Peter 2:15; Jude 11. Balaam loved worldly honor was the reason. P. P. 439-441.

1 Sam. 8:1-5. Samuel's sons were wicked.

1 Sam. 8:6, 7. In rejecting Samuel because his sons were evil, Israel rejected God. P. P. 604, 605.

1 Sam. 15:1-15. Saul changed the testimony.

1 Sam. 15:16-26. Saul was rejected for disobeying the testimony. P. P. 632-635.

1 Kings 14:1-4. Jeroboam tried to deceive an old blind prophet.

1 Kings 14 5-16. Received sad tidings as the result.

Jer. 36:17. Did the secretary write exactly what the prophet said?

Jer. 36:18. The secretary was faithful.

Jer. 36:21-24. Those highest in authority did not respect the testimony. T., v. 5, p. 678.

Jer. 38:4-6. The leading men did not think that the testimonies of Jeremiah were a help to the people. T., v. 5, pp. 79, 76.

Jer. 43:1, 2. The proud men of the church accused the prophet of speaking falsely. T., v. 5, p. 66.

Jer. 43:3. They claimed that the prophet was influenced by Baruch. T., v. 5, pp. 63, 64, 684, 685.

Jer. 29:1. The letters of the prophet are not inspired. T., v. 5, p. 67.

This objection would cast aside a large number of books of the New Testament which are epistles.

1 Cor. 1:10-12. Paul received information from the household of Chloe before he wrote the reproof. T., v. 5, p. 65.

2 Cor. 13:3. Corinthians asked proof that Christ spoke through Paul.

Philemon 9. Paul was aged.

2 Peter 3:15, 16. Paul's writings were hard to

understand. Those who took advantage of this and sought to "wrest," or change, them brought destruction on themselves.

Acts 7:52; Matt. 23:34-37. The people of God have always persecuted the prophets.

Luke 13:33. The world never persecuted a prophet.

Jer. 39:11-14; 40:2-4. The Babylonians took off the chains with which Israel had bound their own prophet.

Hosea 9:8; Mark 6:3, 4. "The prophet is a snare in all his ways." The people see only the humanity in the prophet, and thus reject the message, as the Jews saw "the carpenter's son" in Jesus and rejected Him. Many fail to see divinity in the message from God because it is delivered through a human instrument. T., v. 5, p. 672.

Eccl. 1:9-11; 3:15. History repeats itself.

Old Testament Prophets

Jas. 5:17. Prophets are human beings, subject to the same temptations as other men.

Ex. 3:1. Moses was a shepherd.

1 Sam. 3:1-5; 7:6, 16. Samuel was a priest and judge.

Acts 2:25, 30. David was king.

1 Kings 17:1. Elijah was accustomed to hardships.

1 Kings 19:19-21. Elisha was a farmer.

Amos 1:1. Amos was a herdsman.

Isa. 1:1. Isaiah was the son of Amos.

Jer. 1:1. Jeremiah was a priest.

Eze. 1:1-3. Ezekiel was a priest among the captives of Babylon.

2 Kings 4:8...
    people.

2 Kings 4:38-41; 6:1-7. Elisha spent much time
    with the schools of the prophets.

Jer. 32:6-15. Jeremiah bought land.

1 Kings 13:1-32. Prophets are required to obey
    the words of the Lord spoken by their own
    mouth.

2 Kings 23:15-18. Disobedience on the part of
    the prophet does not hinder the fulfillment
    of the prophecy.

New Testament Prophets

Acts 7:37. Christ was a prophet like Moses,—one
    with whom the Lord spoke "mouth to mouth."
    Num. 12:6-8.

Luke 1:67. Zacharias, the priest, possessed the
    gift of prophecy.

Luke 2:25-27. Simeon, the priest, was a prophet.

Luke 2:36-38. Anna, the prophetess, at the advanced
    age of eighty years published the news of the
    Saviour's birth.

Matt. 11:9-11. John the Baptist, greatest prophet.

Acts 11:27, 28. Agabus prophesied of general
    dearth.

Acts 21:10-12. Seventeen years later he gave a personal testimony to Paul.

Acts 21:8, 9. Philip's four daughters prophesied.

Acts 15:32. Judas and Silas were prophets.

Jas. 5:1-5. The financial condition of the last days revealed through James.

Acts 10:9-17. Peter had visions. Through him was revealed more clearly than by any other prophet the purifying of the earth by fire. 2 Peter 3:7-13.

Rev. 1:10. The book of Revelation portrays the history of the last days as revealed to John in vision. This was given in A. D. 96.

2 Cor. 12:1-7. Paul as late as A. D. 60 speaks of the "abundance of the revelations" that were given him.

THE CONSCIENCE

"Conscience is the voice of God, heard amid the conflict of human passions." T., v. 5, p. 120.

A Good Conscience

Rom. 2:15. The quiet voice within. T., v. 5, p. 512.

Gen. 3:15. Given as a safeguard. T., v. 5, pp. 519, 520.

1 Tim. 1:19. Disregard of conscience means shipwreck. T., v. 5, p. 546.

1 Tim. 1:5. Good conscience and pure heart go together.

1 Peter 3:16. Also good conscience and godly life.

Rom. 2:13-16. Good conscience accords with the law.

Titus 1:1͡5. ͡ ͡ ͡

Titus 1:15. Nothing pure to a defiled conscience.

Titus 1:16, margin. One with defiled conscience
is an unsafe counsellor.

Titus 1:13. Sound in faith, a safeguard against defiled conscience.

2 Tim. 2:16-18, margin. Words from defiled conscience like canker, or gangrene.

Matt. 23:23, 24. They often "strain at a gnat, and
swallow a camel."

Heb. 10:19-23. Only remedy is drawing near to
God.

A Seared Conscience

1 Tim. 4:2. A person may continue in sin until
his conscience is seared. T., v. 2, p. 263.

Eph. 4:19. Given over to lasciviousness and wickedness.

Eph. 4:18. Alienated from the life of God.

1 Tim. 4:2. Hypocrites belong to this class.

Heb. 10:29. Even count the blood of the covenant
unholy.

Consciences Mentioned in the Bible

1 Peter 3:16. Good conscience.

1 Tim. 3:9. Pure conscience.

Heb. 9:14. Purged conscience.

Acts 24:16. Conscience void of offense.
1 Cor. 8:12. Weak conscience. T., v. 4, p. 254;
    v. 2, pp. 90-92.
Heb. 10:22. Evil conscience.
Titus 1:15. Defiled conscience. T., v. 2, p. 42.
1 Tim. 4:2. Seared conscience. T., v. 5, p. 120.

SCHOOLS OF THE PROPHETS

"The schools of the prophets were founded by Samuel, to serve as a barrier against the widespread corruption, to provide for the moral and spiritual welfare of the youth, and to promote the future prosperity of the nation by furnishing it with men qualified to act in the fear of God as leaders and counsellors." P. P. 593.

Location and Finance of the Schools

1 Sam. 19:19, 20. The first school was in Ramah with Samuel as the leading teacher.
1 Sam. 7:1, 2. Kirjath-jearim is thought to be the seat of an important school, as the ark remained there twenty years. E. 46; P. P. 593.
2 Kings 2:3. One school was established in Bethel, no doubt to counteract the worship of the calf that Jeroboam placed in that city.
2 Kings 2:5. Jericho was the seat of another school.
2 Kings 4:38, 43. A school of one hundred students was situated at Gilgal.
2 Kings 6:1-7. Wickedness increased and the last school of the prophets mentioned was removed from the cities and placed in the woods on the banks of the Jordan, where the students would be brought in touch with the elevating

not sufficient, the Lord ...

acle. P. K. 241, 242.

2 Kings 4:38, 39. When they lacked food, instead of complaining or begging, the students gathered wild food.

2 Kings 4:40, 41. By mistake they gathered poison. The Lord cooperated with them in their efforts to sustain themselves and removed the poison from the food. P. K. 240, 241.

2 Kings 4:1-7. One of the students with a family became in debt, and the Lord performed a miracle to pay the debt.

Teachers and Students

1 Sam. 19:20. A leader was appointed to have charge of the schools.

2 Kings 2:3; 1 Sam. 10:12. The leaders were called masters or fathers, and the students were called sons.

1 Kings 18:4; 2 Kings 4:43. The schools were sometimes large.

1 Kings 18:4. The students of the schools of the prophets endured persecution and death rather than compromise the cause of God. P. K. 126.

1 Kings 22:6-14. When the whole company was

swayed by the king, there was yet one prophet true to principle. P. K. 195, 196.

1 Kings 20:35-42; 2 Kings 9:1-10. The students that were true were often sent to transact important business.

2 Kings 6:1. The teacher, or leader, lived with the students. P. K. 260.

2 Kings 6:2, 3. The teachers engaged in manual labor with the students. P. P. 601.

2 Kings 2:16. Manual labor in the schools was conducive to health and vigor. The students were strong men. P. P. 593.

Ps. 74:5. A man's fame consisted in his ability to perform active labor.

2 Kings 4:38-43. The simple vegetarian diet was another interesting feature connected with the schools.

1 Kings 18:4. This simple diet prepared them to face persecution, when they were hidden in the cave, and sustained on bread and water.

Isa. 33:14-17. Before the coming of the Lord, some will be prepared in the same way to pass through a similar experience.

2 Kings 2:3-5. The students were in such close touch with the Lord that they knew when Elijah would be translated. P. K. 225, 226.

2 Kings 2:15. They recognized the presence of the spirit of God, and paid respect to the one guided by the Spirit.

2 Kings 2:23, 24. Surrounded by those who openly ridiculed the good, these young men developed Christian characters.

infinity." D. A. 550; 1., .. -, ,

Degrees of Faith

Heb. 11:6. Faith is an absolute necessity in the Christian life.

Deut. 32:20; 2 Thess. 3:2. The wicked have no faith.

Rom. 12:3. Degrees in Christian character are shown by the measure of faith possessed. D. A. 347.

Luke 12:28. Some have "little faith." M. H. 66.

Rom. 14:1. Others are "weak in faith." C. O. L. 147.

Matt. 15:28. The Syrophenician woman had "great faith." D. A. 400-402.

Acts 11:24. Barnabas was "full of faith."

Luke 17:5. Pray for an increase of faith.

Luke 22:31, 32. Pray that our faith fail not.

Jas. 2:5. Be rich in faith.

2 Tim. 1:5. The faith must be "unfeigned."

2 Peter 1:1. Obtained precious faith.

2 Peter 1:5-8. Faith is the foundation upon which godly character is built. A. A. 529, 530.

Eph. 6:16. Faith will shield us from evil.

Faith a Gift

Heb. 12:2. Jesus is the "author and finisher of our faith." T., v. 5, p. 229.

John 1:1, 14. Christ is the living Word.

Rom. 10:17. Since Christ, the living Word, is the author of our faith, we receive faith by reading the Word. C. O. L. 112.

Eph. 2:8. It is a gift from God, which we receive through the channel of His word.

Jas. 2:18. Faith is shown by our works.

Jas. 2:17. Without work faith dies.

Jas. 2:22. Faith made perfect by works. T., v. 5, p. 200.

Rom. 5:1. Justified by faith.

Rom. 4:5. Faith counted for righteousness.

Gal. 2:16. Faith, not works, justifies.

Jas. 2:24-26. Faith without works will save no one.

Gal. 5:6. Faith works by love.

Eph. 3:17. Faith makes Christ's presence a reality. D. A. 123.

Gal. 2:20. The Christian life is a life of faith. D. A. 389.

Faith that Works

Heb. 11:1, margin. "Faith is the ground, or confidence, of things hoped for, the evidence of things not seen."

Mark 11:24. Faith brings answers to prayers. T., v. 6, p. 467.

Luke 8:43-48. Faith restores diseased organs.

Luke 17:11-19. Faith can restore the body as well as the soul. D. A. 202.

Matt. 6:30-34. The Christian ~~~~~
about temporal things, loses much of the
sweetness of trusting in God. T., v. 6, p. 171.

Matt. 8:23-27. "Little faith" fears the elements.
D. A. 334, 335.

Jas. 5:16-18. Faith can control the elements.

1 Cor. 13:1-3. A faith that can even control the
elements of nature is of no value, unless it
serves as a foundation of a Christian character worked out in daily acts of love.

1 Cor. 13:4-11. A living faith will enable a man
to control his temper.

Jas. 1:26. A working faith will control the tongue.

Door of Faith

Acts 14:27. There is a "door of faith."

Gal. 6:10. When we enter this door, we become
members of the "household of faith."

1 Cor. 16:13. We are to "stand fast in the faith."

2 Cor. 5:7. "We walk by faith." P. K. 175.

1 Thess. 1:3. The Christian will do the "work of
faith." P. K. 164.

1 Tim. 5:8. Some will deny the faith.

1 Tim. 6:10. Love of money will cause some to
err from the faith. P. K. 177.

1 Tim. 6:20, 21. Worldly science will cause some
   to err concerning the faith. P. K. 178.

2 Tim. 3:8. Those of corrupt minds are reprobates
   concerning the faith.

1 Tim. 4:1; 2 Tim. 2:17, 18. Spiritualism and false
   doctrine will cause some to depart from the
   faith.

1 Tim. 1:19, 20. To give up faith means shipwreck of life.

2 Cor. 13:5. We are to examine ourselves to see
   if we are in the faith.

1 Tim. 3:13. A righteous life will have boldness
   in faith.

1 Tim. 6:11, 12. We are to "fight the good fight of
   faith."

Jude 3. Earnestly contend for the faith.

Jude 20. Build ourselves up in the faith. P. K.
   732.

1 John 5:4. Faith will overcome the world. T.,
   v. 5, p. 199.

HEALTH AND TEMPERANCE

"If we carefully preserve the life force, and keep
the delicate mechanism of the body in order, the
result is health." "Without health, no one can as
distinctly understand, or as completely fulfill his
obligations to himself, to his fellow-beings, or to
his Creator. Therefore, the health should be as
faithfully guarded as the character." M. H. 235;
E. 195.

Health

Gen. 43:28; 47:9. Old age alone does not bring
   poor health.

Gen. 48:1, 17-19. Jacob had clear mind in sickness.

from them. T., v. 2, pp. 371, 372.

Ex. 16:3-13. Israel lusted for flesh.

Num. 11:4. Mixed multitude began the complaint.

Num. 11:4-6. Despised food from heaven; wanted flesh.

Num. 11:31-33. With flesh came disease. T., v. 2, pp. 45, 368, 404.

Ps. 78:18; 106:14, 15. Also leanness of soul. T., v. 1, p. 548.

1 Cor. 10:6. We should not lust after evil things as they lusted. T., v. 2, p. 64.

Isa. 4:1. Diet a test of the true church. T., v. 1, pp. 486, 546; v. 6, p. 372.

Diet in Moses' Writings

Gen. 1:29. Nuts, grains, and fruits, original diet.

Gen. 3:17, 18. After sin entered herbs were added to the diet. This diet continued for 1655 years until the flood, or about one-third of the entire history of the world.

Gen. 9:3. After the flood, flesh diet was permitted.

Gen. 9:4. Never allowed to eat blood. A. A. 191-197.

Lev. 7:26, 27. The soul that ate any manner of blood was cut off.

Lev. 17:10-12. No stranger allowed to eat blood.

Acts 15:28, 29. A necessary requirement of the Christian church.

Deut. 12:23-25. Life in the blood.

Lev. 10:17, 18. In some offerings priests ate a portion of the flesh.

1 Sam. 2:12-16. Priests could eat only sodden flesh,—flesh which had been boiled until the blood was extracted from it. The priests that were "sons of Belial," wished raw flesh that could be roasted with the blood in it, thus giving flavor to the flesh. T., v. 6, p. 327; v. 9, pp. 163, 164.

There are many at the present day, who, like the sons of Eli, prefer flesh cooked in a manner to retain the blood. Very little flesh would be eaten if God's requirements were followed. The blood gives flavor. Flesh sodden (put over the fire in cold water and cooked slowly) is almost tasteless.

1 Sam. 2:17. He who disregards the Lord's instruction, whether priest or layman, causes the people to think lightly of the Lord's requirements. T., v. 9, pp. 159, 160.

Lev. 7:23-25. Fat was forbidden. T., v. 2, p. 63.

Lev. 3:17. The command to abstain from blood and fat is a perpetual statute. T., v. 2, p. 61.

Result of Eating Flesh Meat

Gen. 9:5, 6. If man commits murder, the murderer is to be punished by man; but when the beasts are killed to be eaten, God Himself avenges their death.

BEFORE EATING FLESH   **AFTER EATING FLESH**

Name	Age	Age	Name
Adam	930	600	Shem
Seth	912	438	Arphaxad
Enos	905	433	Salah
Cainan	910	464	Eber
Mahalaleel	895	239	Peleg
Jared	962	239	Reu
Enoch	365	230	Serug
Methuselah	969	148	Nahor
Lamech	777	205	Terah
Noah	950	175	Abraham

Noah, the 10th generation, lived 20 years longer than Adam; the 8th generation lived 39 years longer than Adam; Shem was brought up on a vegetarian diet and lived to a fair age; but the 2nd generation after the flood dropped to 438 years; and the 8th generation, instead of being the longest as before the flood, was the shortest,— only 148 years. T., v. 9, p. 156.

Gen. 9:20-23. After eating flesh Noah was drunken.
    T., v. 2, pp. 352, 353.

Gen. 9:25. Curse rested upon descendants.

Prov. 23:20, 21. Drunkenness and flesh-eating associated.

1 Sam. 2:22. Eli's sons, who would have the flesh
with the blood, were licentious. T., v. 2, pp.
62, 352, 362.

Victory in Place of Defeat

Redemption means a re-purchase of that which
was lost. Adam and Eve were not content with
the food God gave them, and coveted forbidden
food; thus they lost Eden. Redeemed man will go
back over the same road and gain victory where
Adam and Eve fell. T., v. 1, pp. 486, 487.

Gen. 3:1-6. Appetite the master of the man Adam,
T., v. 3, p. 161.

Isa. 7:14, 15. The *child* Jesus, through victory
over appetite, able to refuse evil and choose
good.

Matt. 4:3, 4; Luke 4:3, 4. The *man* Jesus, victor
over appetite. T., v. 3, pp. 161, 162.

1 Peter 2:21. Christ left us an example that we
should follow in His steps.

Isa. 4:1-5. In the time of the judgment the members of the apostate church are known by their
choosing their own diet, rather than the diet
given by Christ, the true husband of the
church.

Isa. 66:15-17. Isaiah says that the appetite will
be a test at the coming of Christ. Those who
are ruled by appetite will be destroyed; those
who are victors over appetite will be spared.

Mal. 3:1-6; 4:5, 6. Elijah, a type of the remnant
church. T., v. 6, p. 112; P. K. 227.

1 Kings 17:1-6. He was introduced as a flesh-
eater.

1 Kings 17:9-16. Non-flesh diet next mentioned.

1 Kings 12:1

_... rather than the diseased carcasses of animals?

Swine's Flesh

Gen. 7:2. Division of clean and unclean beasts before the flood. M. H. 280.

Lev. 11:2-28. Scavengers of earth, air, and sea, not to be eaten. T., v. 4, p. 141.

Lev. 11:7, 8. Not to eat or touch swine's flesh. T., v. 2, pp. 62, 94.

2 Peter 2:22: It is a filthy animal. C. T. 48.

Matt. 7:6. Fierce and ungenerous.

Isa. 65:3-5. The eating of swine's flesh is so displeasing to God that He compares it to smoke in His nose.

Isa. 66:15-17. Those found eating swine's flesh when Christ returns will be destroyed. M. H. 313, 314.

Luke 15:15. Herding swine, degrading work.

Mark 5:14-17. Those interested in raising swine, have no interest in Christ or His work. No one can care for swine without violating Lev. 11:7, 8.

Study on 1 Tim. 4:1-7

1 Tim. 4:1. In the last days some depart from the faith of the latter times,—third angel's message.

1 Tim. 4:1-3. They depart from the faith in five definite things:—

1. Give heed to seducing spirits and doctrines of devils,—become spiritualists.

2. Speak lies in hypocrisy.

3. Conscience becomes seared.

4. Forbidding to marry; refuse to be held by the marriage tie; have an affinity for someone besides their lawful companion.

5. Command "to abstain from meats which God created to be received with thanksgiving of them which believe and know the truth."

Every apostate may not be guilty of all of these sins; some may be guilty of one, and others of one or more.

Gen. 1:29. The meats God created for food are fruits, grains, and nuts.

1 Tim. 4:3. Those who believe and know the truth receive this food with thanksgiving, while apostates from the truth of the "latter times," refuse it. T., v. 8, p. 75.

1 Tim. 4:4. Every creature is good for the use for which God created it. Hogs and vultures are good scavengers; but not good for food.

1 Tim. 4:5. Word of God and prayer the test.

1 Tim. 4:6. A good minister of Jesus Christ will warn the brethren against the teaching of these apostates. T., v. 9, pp. 112, 113.

...e freedom from death.

Gen. 25:8; 35:29. There is no mention of sickness
   in recording the death of many of the patriarchs.

Job 2:3, 4. Perfect life does not insure freedom
   from disease.

2 Cor. 12:7. Sickness sometimes draws one nearer
   to God. E. W. 21.

1 Tim. 5:23. Timothy had poor health.

   God permits sickness to draw us nearer to Him;
but often He is disappointed.

Isa. 38:1-8. Hezekiah's sickness and recovery.

Isa. 39:1-8. Instead of magnifying God, he exalted
   himself.

Luke 13:1-5. Sickness not always an evidence of
   sin.

Matt. 8:16, 17. Christ has borne our sickness as
   well as our sins. We may claim freedom from
   disease if it be for God's glory and our good.

Diet and Health

1 Cor. 6:19, 20; Ps. 139:14. Our body God's
   temple. T., v. 6, pp. 375, 376.

1 Cor. 3:16, 17. May be defiled. T., v. 3, p. 163.

Dan. 1:8. Eating improper food defiles the body.

1 Cor. 10:31. Should eat to God's glory. M. H. 305.

Luke 21:34-36. Take heed to the *quantity* and *quality* of food eaten. T., v. 4, pp. 416, 417; v. 2, p. 362.

Eccl. 10:17. Eat in due season for strength. T., v. 4, p. 502.

Isa. 55:2. Money spent for improper food is wasted. Delight in eating good food.

Job 36:16. Set that on your table which is full of fatness. T., v. 9, p. 162; v. 2, pp. 486, 487.

Lev. 7:23. Animal fat forbidden.

Deut. 32:14; Ps. 81:16, margin; 147:14, margin. Eat the fat of kidneys of wheat.

Prov. 23:1-3. Dainties deceitful food. M. H. 302; T., v. 2, pp. 383, 400.

Ps. 103:5. Be satisfied with proper food.

Prov. 15:17; 17:1, 22; Eccl. 9:7. State of mind much to do with appetite.

Isa. 7:14, 15. The Saviour was perfected in childhood by control of appetite, for butter and honey.

The Bible rule for eating honey will apply to all good foods.

Prov. 24:13. Eat honey; it is good.

Prov. 25:16. Be guarded in eating it. T., v. 2, p. 369.

Prov. 25:27. Too much is not good.

Prov. 25:27, 28. The character of the one whose appetite is not controlled is like a city with broken walls; he lacks stability necessary to refuse the evil and choose the good. Isa. 7: 15; T., v. 6, p. 378; M. H. 334.

Matt. 4:1-4. Christ conquered where Adam fell;
all His followers must gain the same victory.
An uncontrolled appetite lost Eden; only controlled appetites can regain it.

Luke 12:35-37. Redeemed eat food in the kingdom of God.

1 Cor. 9:24-27. Temperance principles necessary.
T., v. 6, p. 374.

Appetite

Job 38:39-41. God gave beasts an appetite.

Ps. 104:25-28. He feeds animals.

Matt. 6:25, 26. More interested in food for man.

Deut. 29:18, 19, margin. Do not cultivate any
poisonous plants that will create a thirst.

Deut. 29:20, 21. The one who cultivates such
plants will be separated from God's people.
Tea, coffee, tobacco, and opium are all poisonous herbs that create a thirst; therefore, this
text excludes all of them. T., v. 9, pp. 112, 153;
v. 2, pp. 64, 65, 96, 97.

Luke 1:15. The Holy Spirit does not dwell with
drunkards.

1 Cor. 6:9, 10. No drunkard will enter the kingdom of God.

6

Judges 13:12-14. Mothers should abstain from
    strong drink.

Lev. 10:9, 10. Strong drink perverts the mind;
    cannot discern between right and wrong.

Lev. 10:1, 2. Nadab and Abihu examples.

Dan. 1:8-16. Daniel and his companions risked
    their lives rather than drink the king's wine.

Dan. 1:17-21. Temperate habits made them phys-
    ically, mentally, and spiritually in advance of
    their companions.

Deut. 8:1, 2. Israel's experience was to lead them
    to obey God.

God's Interest in Our Health

Zech. 2:8. God's people are as dear to Him as
    the apple of His eye.

Isa. 53:4, 5. Christ bore our infirmities.

Matt. 8:16, 17. Shown by His healing the sick.

1 Peter 2:24; 3 John 2. Our health as well as for-
    giveness of our sins purchased by the blood
    of Christ.

Matt. 9:36, margin. Christ feels every tired feeling
    of His people.

Ps. 41:3, margin. Regards the sick in mercy.

1 Cor. 6:19, 20. Human body purchased by
    Christ's blood. T., v. 6, p. 369.

Rom. 12:1. Bodies should be a living sacrifice.

2 Cor. 7:1. True sanctification embraces a clean
    body and a pure mind.

Rom. 12:2. Which will not conform to the world.

1 Cor. 10:31. Will eat and drink to God's glory.

Dan. 1:8. Will not defile the body.

1 Cor. 3:16, 17. God destroys those who defile
    the body.

Jas. 5:14-16. Fervent prayer, confession of sins, and anointing with oil, classed together in healing.

Mark 5:23. Hands laid on the sick.

Matt. 17:21. Sometimes fasting as well as prayer required.

Num. 12:13-15. Healing is sometimes deferred till God's lesson is learned.

Job 42:7-10. Job was healed when he prayed for those who had misjudged him.

1 Kings 13:3-6; Luke 17:11-19. Wicked people sometimes healed when God can be glorified thereby.

Fermented Wine

Fermentation is a sign of death, and death is the result of sin. Alcohol is formed by a process of fermentation; hence, it is a direct child of death and sin.

Prov. 20:1. The wine here referred to is fermented; because it is a "mocker" and "deceiver" its character is evil.

Prov. 23:20, 21. This is also fermented wine; for it is evil and is classed with the "riotous" and the "drunkards."

Gen. 9:21. Fermented wine causes one to lose all sense of modesty.

Isa. 5:11. The evil nature of the wine here referred to is revealed in its inflaming the passions.

Isa. 28:7. Fermented wine causes the one who drinks it to err in vision and stumble in judgment.

Prov. 31:4, 5. It will cause one to forget the law and pervert judgment.

Prov. 23:21. The use of it brings poverty.

Prov. 23:29, 30. It brings sorrow and contention.

Eph. 5:18. The use of fermented wine forbidden.

Prov. 23:31. We are forbidden to even look upon this kind of wine.

1 Cor. 6:10. No one addicted to the use of intoxicating wine can enter heaven.

Unfermented Wines

The unfermented wine, or the pure juice of the grape, was used as a beverage from earliest time.

Gen. 40:11. The king of Egypt drank the sweet juice of grapes.

Deut. 32:14. The pure blood of the grape was regarded as a choice drink.

Judges 9:13. It cheers God and man.

Ps. 104:15. Gladdens the heart.

1 Tim. 5:23. It has medicinal qualities.

Mark 2:22. If put in old bottles it ferments, thus becoming unfit for use.

Ex. 12:15. Leaven causes fermentation; at the time of the Passover, all leaven or fermented things were taken away from the homes.

Cooking

Ex. 16:23. Cooking for Sabbath. M. H. 307.

John 21:9-12. Christ cooked food.

1 Kings 19:5-8. Angels have cooked for man.

2 Kings 4:38-41. Elisha directed in the preparation of foods in school of the prophets.

Jer. 7:18. Children helped mothers.

Gen. 18:1-6. Sarah cooked food for angels.

Gen. 25:29-34. Jacob prepared the meal that tempted Esau to sell his birthright.

In Bible times, food was prepared in a variety of ways, as follows: Bread baked in ovens, Lev. 26:26. Also baked on hearths, Gen. 18:6. Sometimes baked on flat plates, 1 Chron. 23:29, margin. Badly baked bread, type of sin, Hosea 7:8. Seethed food is boiled, Eze. 24:5. Food roasted, Ex. 12:9. Grain parched, Ruth 2:14. Green corn dried, Lev. 2:14. Fruit dried, 1 Sam. 25:18. Fruit juice bottled air tight, Luke 5:37, 38. Vegetable soup, 2 Kings 4:38-41. Fish broiled, Luke 24:42.

Simplicity of Diet

Gen. 18:1-8. Angel given meal with four varieties of food.

Gen. 25:33, 34. Jacob's tempting meal was bread and lentil soup.

Ruth 2:14. Boaz gave his men three varieties.

1 Sam. 30:11, 12. Bread, dried fruit, and water, refreshed a faint and hungry man.

1 Kings 17:13, 14, margin. Elijah had only bread and oil for a full year.

1 Kings 19:6, 7. The angel gave him bread and water.

2 Kings 4:38-42. Vegetable soup, barley bread, and corn, food at school of prophets.

Matt. 14:19. The Saviour fed the multitude two varieties.

John 21:9, 12. Two varieties in the meal the Saviour cooked.

If the meals in our homes were more often after the Bible plan, there would be less dyspepsia, and the tired housewives would have more time to study their Bibles. T., v. 2, p. 367.

Conservation of Food

John 6:12. Save every fragment of food. M. H. 48; T., v. 5, p. 400.

Isa. 59:7. Wastefulness is classed with wickedness.

Prov. 23:2, 3; Luke 21:34. Caution against gluttony, or surfeiting.

Prov. 18:9. A great waster is brother to the slothful. M. H. 195.

Prov. 6:6-8. Gather food in the summer for winter use. M. H. 299; T., v. 7, p. 134.

Prov. 30:25. Physical weakness is no excuse for failure to provide food for winter use.

Gen. 41:28-36. God directed that food be gathered for famine in time of plenty.

Mark 2:22. The Saviour indorsed the custom of sealing up fruit juice.

..... 12, Luke 12:1; 1 Cor.
5:6, 7; Hosea 7:4.

Shewbread. Ex. 25:23-30; 40:22; 2 Chron. 2:4;
1 Chron. 9:32; Lev. 24:5-8; 1 Sam. 21:6;
Lev. 24:9; 1 Sam. 21:3, 4; John 6:32-34,
53-63.

Interesting incidents connected with bread in Bible history. Judges 7:13-15; 1 Kings 17:6, 14-16, margin; 2 Kings 4:42-44; Joshua 9:3-14; Matt. 4:3, 4; Mark 6:37-44; 8:2-9; Luke 24: 30, 31, 35; Matt. 26:26; 6:9-15; Isa. 33:16, 17.

Butter

Dr. Benisch, in his Hebrew Bible, uses the term "clotted cream" instead of butter in the following texts where it refers to food: Gen. 18:8; Deut. 32:14; Judges 5:25; 2 Sam. 17:29; Job 20:17; Isa. 7:15, 22.

"Butter" is used figuratively in Ps. 55:21; Job 29:6, and Prov. 30:33. Butter anciently was not a common article of food as at the present day. The Greeks and Romans used it only for medicinal purposes.

Preserving Food for Winter Use

Ant an example. Prov. 6:6-8; Job 12:7; Prov. 30:25.

Dried. 2 Sam. 16:1; 1 Sam. 25:18; Lev. 2:14.

Bottled. 2 Sam. 16:1; Matt. 9:17.

Parched. Ruth 2:14; 1 Sam. 17:17.

DRESS

"The Bible teaches modesty of dress. . . . Any device designed to attract attention to the wearer or to excite the admiration, is excluded from the modest apparel which God's word enjoins." M. H. 287.

Dress of a Christian

Heb. 2:10. Christ the captain of our salvation.

2 Tim. 2:3, 4. True Christians good soldiers.

Eph. 6:10-17; 1 Peter 5:8, 9. A real warfare. Contending armies always have different uniforms. T., v. 4, pp. 628-647.

Gen. 3:7. When Adam and Eve were wholly under the control of Satan, they dressed according to his mind. The dress did not properly cover either the upper or lower part of the body.

Gen. 3:15, 21. When God placed enmity in their hearts against the devil, He changed their manner of dress and *clothed* them; God did not accept them in His service half clothed.

Num. 15:38, 39. When one joins the army of the Lord, he should dress differently from the world. T., v. 3, p. 366.

Isa. 3:16-24. Everyone of these fashions is the height of style in some part of the earth.

Judges 8:24. Ishmaelites wore earrings.

Isa. 3:16. The haughty have always worn these ornaments of the world.

Prov. 7:10; Gen. 38:15. Harlots are known by their dress.

2 Kings 9:30; Eze. 23:40 ...
face, and tire...

...of Christ's

...own righteousness is as filthy rags.
...ut. 22:11. The Israelites were forbidden to make
a garment of two different kinds of mate-
rial, thus teaching that self-righteousness could
not be mingled with the robe of Christ's righteousness.

Lev. 13:47-57. If the leprosy was in the "warp or
in the woof" of a garment, it must be burned.
No one allowed to wear a garment that endan-
gered the lives of others. Leprosy a type of
sin. The most insidious sin is pride, which
caused the downfall of Lucifer. Eze. 28:17.

The dress of the world is made to foster pride.
Garments of that kind should not be worn by
Christians. Professed Christians may say that the
garments are given them; and that they are not
proud, and think there is no harm in wearing them;
but there is contagion in the garments, and they
may be a stumbling-block to others, and cause their
spiritual death. T., v. 4, p. 640.

Lev. 13:58. If the garment can be altered so as not
to represent the world, it is safe for the Christian to wear it.

Num. 15:39. A Christian's dress should remind him
of God's law.

Gen. 34:1, 2. Jacob allowed Dinah to mingle with
the young people of the world.

Gen. 34:4-31. Disgrace and shame followed.

Gen. 35:1-4. Then Jacob had his household *change
their garments* and take off their ornaments.
T., v. 4, p. 647.

If Dinah had dressed as God designs His people
to dress, she would not have been invited to mingle
with the princes and princesses of the land. God
designs the plain dress of His people to be a safeguard against many snares of the enemy. Plainly
dressed young people escape many temptations that
come to those who wear the uniform of the world.
T., v. 3, p. 376.

Joshua 7:21. Men as well as women like worldly
attire.

Matt. 23:5. Jesus reproved the priests for catering
to pride.

Various Instructions Regarding Dress

Deut. 22:5. Women shall not wear men's clothing;
neither men put on women's garments.

Prov. 31:21, margin. Extra clothing should be
worn in winter. M. H. 293.

Acts 12:8. Dress properly in night air.

1 Tim. 2:9. Christians should wear *modest* apparel, instead of the *immodest* dress of the
world, exposing the limbs and breast.

1 Tim. 2:9. Costly ornaments should be eliminated.
M. H. 207, 287.

Rev. 17:4, 5. Such ornaments become the harlot,
but not the professed Christian.

Rev. 19:8. True Christians, knowing that God

has taken garments as a typ...

can not be ch...

...ded from the

...rom the soft, yielding waist.

... 292.

All Christians should dress *modestly, healthfully, tastefully, and neatly,* thus representing the principles of the heavenly kingdom. T., v. 2, pp. 66, 610-614; E. 248.

ORDINANCES OF THE CHURCH

"The ordinances of baptism and the Lord's supper are two monumental pillars; one without and one within the church. Upon these ordinances Christ has inscribed the name of the true God." T., v. 6, p. 91.

Baptism

"Apart from Christ, baptism, like any other service, is a worthless form."

Eph. 4:5. One baptism.

Heb. 6:2. Doctrine of baptism.

Acts 2:38. When one repents, is cleansed by the blood of Christ, and baptized, he receives the baptism of the Holy Ghost.

1 John 5:8. It is then that "the spirit, and the water, and the blood" bear witness in earth.

John 3:23. Much water required.

Acts 8:36. Must go to the water.

Acts 8:38. Both candidate and administrator go down into the water. A. A. 108, 109.

Matt. 3:16; Acts 8:39. After baptism they come out of the water. D. A. 111.

Rom. 6:4; Col. 2:12. Memorial of Christ's burial.

Rom. 6:3-11. Must be dead to sin. T., v. 6, p. 93.

Rom. 6:1-5. A pledge of the resurrection.

John 3:5; Rom. 6:4-6; Col. 2:12, 13. A birth to a new life. A. A. 475, 476.

Eph. 5:26; Acts 22:16. Outward type of inward cleansing.

Matt. 28:19. In the name of the Trinity. T., v. 6, p. 91.

Gal. 3:27; Rom. 6:3. Baptized into Christ. T., v. 9, pp. 133, 155.

Acts 10:48; 19:5, margin. Into the name of Christ. Baptism is the door of the church. T., v. 6, pp. 98, 99.

1 Peter 3:21; Mark 16:16. Salvation in baptism; it is the answer of a good conscience.

Acts 8:39. Brings rejoicing.

Ordinance of Humility

John 13:1-4. Instituted after the Passover supper.

John 13:5. Jesus washed the disciples' feet.

John 13:6-9. Peter felt unworthy until he found that it was necessary. D. A. 646.

John 13:10, 11. This was Judas' last call. D. A. 645.

John 13:12, 13. Jesus asked if they knew what He had done.

John 13:14. "If I then your Lord and Master,

have washed your feet, ye alone another's feet." F
John 13:15. "W

...nce of hu-
...er the Passover sup-
...they partook of the bread and
...for as soon as they finished the communion, they sung an hymn and went out.

1 Tim. 5:10. It was celebrated in the early Christian church.

The Lord's Supper

1 Cor. 11:23. Instituted Thursday evening, the
night before Christ's betrayal. D. A. 652.

1 Cor. 11:23, 24. Bread symbol of Christ's body.
D. A. 653.

1 Cor. 11:25. Wine represents the blood of Christ.

1 Cor. 11:26. A reminder of Christ's second coming. D. A. 659.

1 Cor. 11:27, 29. A sin to eat unworthily.

1 Cor. 11:29, 30. Sickness and death the result of
not discerning the Lord's body. D. A. 660.

1 Cor. 11:28. All should examine themselves. D. A.
656.

Matt. 26:20-28. Not criticize others, but say, "Lord,
is it I?"

Matt. 26:29. The Saviour is refraining from drink-

ing the fruit of the vine until all get home
in the kingdom.

Acts 2:46. Bread broken daily in the early
church.

Acts 20:7-11. Paul broke bread between midnight
and daybreak.

The ordinance is very sacred but can be celebrated at any time.

Tithe

"Voluntary offerings and the tithe constitute the
revenue of the gospel."

Ps. 24:1. God owns everything. P. P. 526.

Deut. 8:18. All wealth comes from God. T., v. 5,
p. 150.

Matt. 25:14. We are stewards of the Lord's goods.
T., v. 5, p. 382.

Lev. 27:32. All substance divided into ten parts;
one-tenth kept by God. T., v. 3, p. 394; E.
250.

Lev. 27:30. It is *holy*; it does not belong to man.

Mal. 3:8. He who uses the tithe for himself, robs
God. T., v. 3, p. 269.

Lev. 27:31. If used, add "the fifth part thereof."

Lev. 27:33. An honest tithe is one-tenth, whether
it be much or little.

Joel 2:17. The priest and those that ministered
about holy things were the Lord's servants.

Num. 18:20-24. The Lord supported them with the
tithe.

Acts 13:2-4. God selects His own workers now as
anciently.

1 Cor. 9:8-13. Those who work in spiritual lines are
supported by carnal things.

1 Cor. 9:14. As the priests in the temple were

supported by the tithe, "even so ...
ordained that they ...
should li...

M...

... honest tithe-payer is

Offerings

Mal. 3:8. Required.

Prov. 3:9, 10; Ex. 23:19. Give the best.

Matt. 6:1-4. In God's sight only.

Haggai 1:5-11. Curse on covetousness.

Luke 6:38. God a good pay-master.

2 Cor. 9:6-15. Cheerful giver loved.

Prov. 19:17. Give to the poor.

Church Organization

"Never allow anyone's ideas to unsettle your faith in regard to order and harmony which should exist in the church." T., v. 5, p. 274.

Deut. 1:15. Ancient organization same as the present.

God is the center of all organization: next to God stands His prophet, or mouthpiece; then follows:—

1. Leader "over thousands,"—General Conference.
2. Leader "over hundreds,"—union conferences.
3. Leader "over fifties,"—local conferences.
4. Leader "over tens,"—churches.

Besides, officers or secretaries to attend to the

different branches of the work. E. 37; A. A. 93, 94.

1 Cor. 14:33, 40. Order in the Christian church. A. A. 163, 164, 185, 186.

1 Tim. 4:14. Ministers ordained by the presbytery. A. A. 18, 161, 162, 503, 504.

1 Cor. 16:1, 2. Uniform system throughout the churches. A. A. 91, 270, 317, 318.

Acts 15:1-4. Perplexing questions referred from local churches to the conference. A. A. 195-197.

Acts 15:1-4. Council held at the head of the work.

Acts 15:23-25. Report of decision sent to all the churches.

Acts 15:30, 31. Document first read in the church where the trouble arose.

Acts 16:1, 4, 5. Afterwards read in other churches.

Acts 8:26, 29; 19:21, 22. While there was perfect organization, yet each worker was free to work as God directed. A. A. 164, 200, 405.

Titus 1:5. Churches could not ordain their own local elders.

ORGANIZATION OF LOCAL CHURCHES

Officers

Titus 1:5. Elders or bishops. A. A. 95, 96.

1 Tim. 3:13. Deacons. A. A. 88, 89.

Rom. 16:1, 2. Deaconess (Alford's Translation).

Phil. 1:1. Sometimes more than one elder, also more than one deacon.

Duty of Elders, or Bishops

1 Tim. 3:1-3. Blameless character, apt to teach.

1 Tim. 3:4, 5. Good control over his own household and children.

1 Tim. 3:7. Must be respected by ~~peo~~
the church.

~~Ti~~

..........., those who
.... their conscience.

1 Tim. 3:12. Must control their own children and
households.

1 Tim. 3:10. Proved before they are ordained.

1 Tim. 3:13; Acts 6:8. Faithful deacons are valuable workers. T., v. 5, p. 304.

Duty of Deaconesses

Rom. 16:1, 2. Attend to business connected with
the church, especially to succor those in need.

PROMISES OF GOD

"All the promises of God in Him (Christ) are
yea, and in Him amen unto the glory of God by
us." 2 Cor. 1:20; 2 Peter 1:4.

Below are some of the promises given for various
conditions in life.

SINNER. Rom. 5:8, 6; 1 Tim. 1:15; 1 Peter 3:18;
Isa. 1:18; 1 John 1:9, 7; Eph. 2:4, 5, 8; John
16:7, 8; Eph. 4:17-25; 1 John 3:4; Ps. 37:31;
Isa. 43:25, 26; 61:10.

CHRISTIAN. 1 Cor. 10:13; 1 Peter 4:12, 13, 16;
Isa. 41:10, 11, 13-15; 1 Peter 3:12; Isa. 43:2,
3; Ps. 91:15; Isa. 49:25; Matt. 6:6; Jas.

1:5-8; Luke 11:9-13; Ps. 91:9, 10; Rev. 3:10; Ps. 34:7; Rev. 22:14.

OVERCOMER. 1 John 5:4; Rev. 2:7, 11, 17, 26-28; 3:5, 12, 21.

BACKSLIDER. Jer. 2:19, 20; 3:12, 13; Hosea 14:2; Jer. 29:13, 11; 31:3; Jer. 3:14, 22; Hosea 14:4, 5; 6:1.

YOUNG. Prov. 8:17; 1 John 2:13, 14; Prov. 20:29; Ps. 119:9.

AGED. Ps. 92:13, 14; Prov. 16:31; 20:29; Ps. 71:9, 18; Isa. 46:4; Ps. 48:14; 116:15.

WIDOW. Jer. 49:11; Prov. 15:25; Ps. 68:5, 6; 146:9.

ORPHAN. Prov. 23:10; Jer. 49:11; Hosea 14:3; Ps. 10:14; 68:5.

MOURNER. Matt. 5:4; Isa. 66:13.

DIET AND DRESS

Apparel of the Apostate Wife of Christ

Isa. 3:16-24. Fashions of the world.
Isa. 64:6. Self-righteousness.

Apparel of the True Wife of Christ

1 Peter 3:1-5. Free from unnecessary adornments.
1 Tim. 2:9, 10. Modest apparel.
Isa. 61:10. Robe of righteousness.

Diet of Apostate Wife of Christ

Isa. 65:3, 4; 66:17. Swine's flesh.
Isa. 22:12-14. Flesh of sheep and oxen.
Prov. 23:20. Wine and flesh.
Prov. 23:29-32. Mixed wine.
Eze. 22:26-28. Traditions.

Diet of the True Wife of Christ

Gen. 1:29. Fruits, nuts and grains.

Lev. 11:1-28. Clean food.

John 6:51, 63. Feed on th͟—͟

Ps. 119:103. Go͟d͟—͟

͟—͟ charm

͟—͟—͟

͟—͟ to show kindness to any

͟—͟ave physical deformities, as the blind, deaf, etc.

Ex. 22:22-24. Be kind to those who have passed through heavy sorrow, widows and fatherless children.

2 Tim. 2:24. "Be gentle unto all men." P. K. 237; T., v. 2, p. 647.

1 Peter 3:7. Men should respect and honor the women.

1 Tim. 2:12, 13. Women should not be forward and take the place of men, but should recognize men as occupying the first place.

Matt. 5:33-37. Avoid *all* slang expressions of every sort. C. O. L. 336, 337.

Prov. 7:11. Avoid all loud talking. M. H. 489, 490.

Prov. 6:13-15. Winking, or making signs with the hands and feet, is very rude.

Prov. 25:17. It is not good etiquette to visit the same family too often.

Prov. 27:14. If one rises very early in the morning,

he should be quiet so as not to disturb others.

1 Peter 3:1-5. Nothing adds to a woman's charms like a "meek and quiet spirit." T., v. 2, p. 133.

Prov. 31:30. "Favor is deceitful, and beauty is vain, but a woman that feareth the Lord, she shall be praised."

TEMPTATION

Jas. 1:13. God tempts no one.

1 Chron. 21:1. The devil is the author of temptation.

Jas. 1:14. We are tempted through our lusts.

1 Tim. 6:9, 10. Covetousness causes many to fall.

Matt. 4:4, 7, 10. Temptation can be resisted by the word of God.

1 Cor. 10:13. God will not suffer His people to be tempted above what they are able to bear.

2 Peter 2:9. God knows how to deliver the godly out of temptation.

LESSONS FROM NATURE

Many beautiful lessons can be drawn from the following texts:

RAIN. Gen. 2:6; Job 5:8-10; 36:26-28; Gen. 7:11, 12; Job 37:14-16; Jer. 14:22; Ps. 147:7, 8; Jer. 5:23, 24; Job 28:25, 26; Deut. 11:17; Jer. 3: 2, 3; Amos 4:7; 1 Kings 17:1; Jas. 5:17, 18; 1 Kings 18:41-46; Gen. 7:4, 12; 1 Sam. 12: 17, 18; 1 Kings 18:45; Ezra 10:9, 13; Isa. 55:10, 11; Deut. 32:1, 2; Ps. 72:6; Joel 2:23; Ps. 68:9; Eze. 34:26; Zech. 10:1; Isa. 44:3, 4; Lev. 26:4.

DEW. Prov. 3:19, 20; Job 38:28; Gen. 27:28;

Luke 9:22. "Be raised the th...
Luke 18:33. "The third d...
Luke 24:7. "The third...
Mark 9:31. "He ...
Luke 24:46. ...
  day ...

...sday
...be the evening
...nvered Himself into the ...
from that time He was in ...
8:31. Christ said He would be ...
elders, and of the chief priests, and ...
be *killed,* and *after three days* rise again ...
time *before* the angry mob came to arrest Hi...
had been "rejected," otherwise they would nev...
have gathered to take Him. "After three days" ...
had passed from the time of His *rejection,* He rose
again. Christ was arrested Thursday evening; the
trial lasted all night. At noon on Friday He was
crucified. He died about three o'clock in the afternoon, and rested in the tomb until the third day.

The Jews asked for a sign. Matt. 12:38-40. After
saying the wicked ask for signs, Christ said that
they should have the sign of Jonas the prophet.

45;
6:4.

LIGHTNING. E...
16; Job 28:26; ...
Eph. 2:2; Job 1:12, ...
10:18; Rev. 4:5; 8:5; Rev. ...
24:27; Ps. 97:4-6; 77:18; Dan. ...
3; Eze. 1:14. ...

Gen. 8:1; Amos 4:13; Job 1:1, 19; ...
135:7; Jer. 51:16; Ps. 147:18; Is. 11:15; ...
Job 28:25; Ex. 10:13, 14:21; Num. 11:31; Ps. 148:
22:11; Ps. 27:8; Ps. 104:3; Zech. 7:14; Dan.
7, 8; Mark 4:37-39; Isa. 32:2; Jas. 1:6, 7;
11:40; Matt. 7:24, 25; Dan. 7:2; Eze. 37:9, 10; Prov.
25:14; John 3:8; Acts 2:2; Eccl. 11:4; Eze. 13:11, 18;
Dan. 2:35; Isa. 32:2.

SAND. Gen. 22:17; 32:12; Jer. 5:22; Heb. 11:
12; Ps. 139:17, 18.

ROCK. Deut. 32:4; 2 Sam. 22:2; Ps. 18:2; 31:2,
3; margin; Isa. 32:2; 1 Cor. 10:4; Ps. 78:16;
Num. 20:8; Ex. 33:22; Matt. 21:44.

RIVERS. Gen. 2:10; Isa. 48:18; 66:12; Ps. 1:
1-3; Jer. 17:7, 8; Rev. 22:1, 2; Ps. 46:4;

CLOUDS. Lev. 16:2; Ex. 14:20; 19:9; 1 Kings
8:12; Ps. 18:11, 12; 1 Kings 18:41-46; Ps.
36:5; 57:10; Ps. 68:34; 77:17; Job 36:29; 37:
14-16; Ps. 104:3; Job 37:21; Rev. 14:14; Jude

RAINBOW. Gen. 9:13-15; Eze. 1:28; Rev. 4:3;
Gen. 9:14, 16; Jer. 29:11-14.

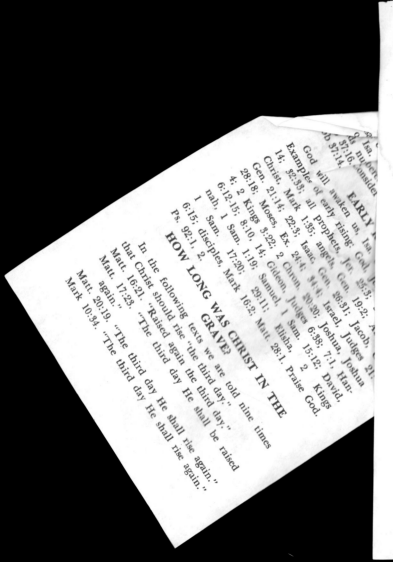

(rotated inset page)

as nu... consider
Isa. 57:16; Job 37:14.

God will awaken us. Isa.

Examples of early rising: God, ...
14; 32:33; all prophets, Jer. 25:3; A...
Christ, Mark 1:35; angels, Gen. 19:2; A...
Gen. 21:14; 22:3; Isaac, Gen. 26:31; Jacob,
28:18; Moses, Ex. 24:4; Israel, Judges
4; 2 Kings 3:22; 2 Chron. 20:20; Joshua, Joshua
6:12,15; 8:10, 14; Gideon, Judges 6:38; 7:1, Han-
nah, 1 Sam. 1:19; Samuel, 1 Sam. 15:12; David,
1 Sam. 17:20; disciples, Mark 16:2; Matt. 28:1. Praise God.
6:15; Ps. 92:1, 2.

HOW LONG WAS CHRIST IN THE GRAVE?

In the following texts we are told nine times
that Christ should rise "the third day."
Matt. 16:21. "Raised again the third day."
Matt. 17:23. "The third day He shall be raised
again."
Matt. 20:19. "The third day He shall rise again."
Mark 10:34. "The third day He shall rise again."

"As Jonas was three days and three nights in the whale's belly, so shall the Son of man be three days and three nights in the heart of the earth." If we take this language literally as it reads, we must understand that Christ spent three days and three nights in the heart, or center, of the earth; but the tomb of Joseph in which the Saviour lay was on the surface of the ground in plain sight. The term "earth" is often used when referring to the people on the earth. Jer. 6:19; Isa. 1:2. From the evening Christ delivered Himself into the hands of the mob until He came forth a mighty conqueror, He was in the hands of the people; the "heart of the earth."

This is according to the words of the angel: "The Son of man must be delivered into the hands of sinful men, and be crucified, and the third day rise again." Luke 24:4-7. He rose the third day after He delivered Himself "into the hands of sinful men."

EVERY-DAY TOPICS

Rich spiritual lessons can be gained from the following groups of texts: D. A. 476, 477.

SWEEPING. There are eight texts which speak of sweeping. A careful study of these texts aid in sweeping sin from our lives that we may never be swept from the earth by the Lord's besom of destruction. Judges 5:21; Jer. 46:15; Prov. 28:3; Isa. 14:23; 28:17; Matt. 12:43, 44; Luke 11:25; 15:8-10.

WASHING DISHES. Poorly done illustrates a hypocrite, Matt. 23:25, 26. Thorough work

1 Thess. 2:19, 20;

Anyone who has not
soul cannot enter into the

MANY CROWNS

Rev. 19:12

n of life, Rev. 2:10. Of gold, Rev. 14:14.
glory, 1 Peter 5:4. Of righteousness, 2 Tim.
4:8. Of rejoicing, 1 Thess. 2:19. Of lovingkindness, Ps. 103:4. Of glory and honor, Heb. 2:7,
9. Of knowledge, Prov. 14:18. Incorruptible, 1 Cor.
9:25.

CHARACTERISTICS OF MELCHISEDEC

1. Like unto the Son of God.   2. Priest of the
Most High God.   3. Abideth a priest continually.
4. King of Salem. 5. King of righteousness. 6.
King of peace.   7. Greater than Abraham.   8.
Without father. 9. Without mother. 10. Without